OOMPH POWER!

How to Get Re-Energized for Outrageous Success

Susan Miller

Simpson Wesley
PUBLISHERS

First Printing 2003

Library of Congress Cataloging-In-Publication Data

Miller, Susan

Oomph power!: how to get re-energized for outrageous success/ by Susan Miller.. – 1st ed.
p. cm.

Includes bibliographical references.

ISBN: 0-9740686-0-8
LCCN: 2003092065
1. Motivation 2. Success in business
3. Relationships I. Title.

Book edited by Susan Stanley
Book designed by Sue Schaefer, GetSET

This book is dedicated

in loving memory of my father,

Paul Wesley Kihm.

Acknowledgments

Special thanks go first and foremost to my editor Susan Stanley who **oomph**ed me on from the start and kept me going and going.

My never-ending gratitude and love to my husband, Steve and my sister, Kathleen Kihm for their constant help and encouragement, and to my mother, Louise Kihm, especially for calling me, "my daughter, the author."

I am so grateful to:
Coach Rick Pitino and Vincent Tatum for their terrific help and support.
Vicki Lenz for her many suggestions and early faith in the book.
Paula Kommor and Cathy Hinko for their immensely helpful early draft critiques.
Marolyn Wright for being the first and most valuable supporter of my speaking career.
Father Bill Griner, Church of the Epiphany, and Paul Long, Yoga East, for giving me spiritual **oomph**.

I am blessed with wonderful friends and family who re-energized me and responded to my frequent requests for feed-back: Nan Hazel, Sandi and Alan Bryant, Nancy Swigonski, M.D., Ellen Friedman, Sandy Wagner, the Riley-Kline family, Barkley Payne, Carol Hensley, Ken Herndon, Kim Kolarik, Gail Iwaniak, Sara Parks, John Henderson, Helen Shown, Dave Eggleston, Molly Mugglestone, Anne Duncan, Judy Noland, Tiffany Miller, Teresa Dreckman, Vicki Arrowood, Meg Fuqua, Deidre Lark, Ann McArthur, Cathi Peters, Ann Roman, Douglas Kihm and Carol Schreiber.

A special thank you to these fellow speakers for their generous help: Conway Stone, Larry Winget, Lee Silber, David Eastman, Joe Bonura, Linda Larsen, Meryl Runion, Bob Wade, Terry Lubotsky, Rosina Harter, and SkillPath "Den Mom" Claudia Mayorga.

And a huge thank you to each and every person who has ever attended one of my speeches or seminars. This book's for *you*!

Contents

Preface

This picture depicts what this book is all about. That's my older sister Kathy on the left and I'm the topless tyke fishing in a rain puddle in front of our house. Even at age two, I believed:

☞ **Dream big.... Anything is possible!**

☞ **Concentrate on the job at hand.**

☞ **Don't just do it.... Do it with oomph!**

Fifty years later, I live beside a river instead of a puddle, I am blessed with outrageous success and my list of three beliefs has grown to over sixty principles I teach and live by.

I wrote this book because people have always remarked on how much energy I have. They ask where I get my enthusiasm and what I'm "on." Someone once said I probably get speeding tickets even when I'm parked! I admit I *am* super-perky, highly energetic and even "hyper-enthusiastic," as once described by a journalist.

But I am not *always* energetic and on fire with enthusiasm. In fact, it took me almost five years to finish this book. Why? Because when it came to this one project, I got "stuck" and wasn't practicing the principles I preached.

I believe we all start out full of **oomph**—energy and enthusiasm—for our jobs, our relationships, for our projects. But the **Oomph** Busters I describe in Chapter Four begin to deplete that energy and we sometimes get bogged down or stuck in a rut.

That is why this book focuses on how to get re-energized for outrageous success. It doesn't just assert, "Have a positive attitude;" it tells you specifically HOW to re-energize your attitude. These strategies have worked for me and I know they will for you, too!

I went to a bookstore and asked the saleswoman where the self-help section was. She said if she told me, it would defeat the purpose. *George Carlin*

Introduction

I began writing this book five years ago, but it languished unfinished while I traveled **a lot**, speaking at seminars and conferences from Auckland, New Zealand to Akron, Ohio. Then, six months ago, I realized I had told thousands of people in my audiences that some day ***soon*** they would see me on Oprah talking about **Oomph Power!** Feeling accountable to these people, I began to systematically practice the **oomph** boosters I was writing about.

My "writer's block" magically disappeared and the book almost wrote itself. I'm here to tell you, this stuff works. Now I just have to get booked on Oprah!

I wrote this book for anyone who has ever felt "stuck" like me and wants to get ***re-energized*** to enjoy outrageous success in their personal and professional lives.

Because I am the most impatient person in the world, I will not bore you with long explanations and flowery phrasing. **Oomph Power!** is short on theory and long on practical, how-to techniques.

As a motivational speaker and seminar leader, I have read countless books and hundreds of magazine articles on motivation, stress control, interpersonal skills and self-esteem. I have spoken to thousands of people around the world and have collected energizing tips from my audience members and from the experts.

These serious, funny and thought-provoking points of wisdom are interspersed throughout the book. You may want to highlight the ones that resonate for you or create a screen saver for your computer from your favorite quote.

These are my principles...and if you don't like them, I have others.

Groucho Marx

But reading or saying motivational platitudes is not enough to get you re-energized, re-charged and unstuck. You have to take action!

The DO THIS! action items can help you form new habits. Benjamin Franklin would list 52 faults he wanted to eliminate or virtues he wanted to cultivate at the beginning of each year. He then worked on a different one each week. You can follow Ben's ambitious plan or just choose the action items **you** want to practice. Remember that it takes 21 days to make a new habit or break an old one.

We are what we repeatedly do. Excellence then is not an act but a habit. *Aristotle*

You can read this book cover-to-cover or pick the topic that interests you the most and make that your starting point. I have AAADD (Age-Activated Attention Deficit Disorder) so the book is written in easy-to-read "info-bites."

I hope you will pick-up **Oomph Power**! whenever you feel your energy or enthusiasm waning or you feel stuck in a rut and need some instant **oomph.**

Let's get started!

Chapter One

What Is Oomph Power?

(And Why You Need It for Outrageous Success)

I believe knowledge, talent and desire are all factors of success. But nine times out of ten, the job, the promotion, the sale, the great relationship, the *whatever,* goes to the person who is more energetic and enthusiastic—the person with **oomph!**

Oomph, as defined in the dictionary, means "energy, enthusiasm, vitality." The opposite of **oomph** is dullness, mediocrity and indifference.

When all other factors are equal, a little **oomph** will put you over the top. That's **Oomph Power!**

Nothing great was ever accomplished without enthusiasm!

Ralph Waldo Emerson

I believe people succeed in direct proportion to how much enthusiasm they have for who they are, what they do and for whom they are with.

The English word "enthusiasm" comes from the Greek word "entheos" which means "the god or inspiration within us." In other words, enthusiasm is an "inside job" and can't be easily faked.

Enthusiastic people—people with **oomph**—are excited about life and it shows! Enthusiasm is like a pot of boiling water with the lid on. The pot doesn't have to boil over for you to know the energy is there; you can see it and feel it. It's the same with people. When I am with a person with **oomph**, whether I am having a great day or a lousy one, I always end up feeling re-energized. Enthusiasm and energy are contagious!

A man can succeed at almost anything for which he has unlimited enthusiasm.

Charles Schwab

Quantum physicists have documented how the brain has electrical energy that gives off varying vibrations depending upon thoughts and moods. Because "like energy attracts like energy," it follows that positivity might attract positive results. It may be why the rich get richer, misery loves company and why, when you've already got a sweetie, it's easier to <u>attract</u> a sweetie!

ENTHUSIASM

You can do anything if you have
enthusiasm.
Enthusiasm is the yeast that makes
your hopes rise to the stars.
Enthusiasm is the sparkle in your
eyes, the swing in your gait, the
grip of your hand,
the irresistible surge of will and
energy to execute your ideas.
Enthusiasts are fighters.
They have fortitude.
They have staying qualities.
Enthusiasm is at the bottom of all
progress.
With it, there is accomplishment.
Without it, there are only alibis.

Henry Ford

What is Outrageous Success?

The word outrageous is defined as: "extreme, outside the norm, shocking, beyond what anyone thinks is possible." Success simply means: reaching your goals. Your goals are everything you want to be, have and do.

If you have ordinary, average, run-of-the-mill **goals**, you will only have ordinary, average, run-of-the-mill success.

If you have ordinary, average, run-of-the-mill **enthusiasm** for what you want, you will only have ordinary, average, run-of-the-mill success.

For outrageous success, you must reach above the ordinary, the mediocre and the average. Dream big! What do you **really** want?

We're not here to stick our toe in the water. We're here to make waves!

Outrageous success is not about having all the money in the world. It's not "whoever dies with the most toys wins." Outrageous success is enjoyed by whoever has the most time to *play* with their toys *and* has the most **fun** playing with them.

Outrageous success is about experience, not ownership. If you are not happy *inside,* then nothing *outside* you will ever make you happy. Outrageous success means having relationships that bring you happiness. Outrageous success means you *really* look forward to each new day and help other people do the same.

Success is living up to your potential. That's all. Wake up with a smile and go after life...Live it, enjoy it, taste it, smell it, feel it.

Joe Kapp

So, outrageous success means reaching *your* goals, whatever they may be. Yet, when I do the goal-setting exercise outlined in Chapter Three in my seminars, I find many people have a hard time even describing their goals. Instead, they focus on their limitations: why they can<u>not</u> be, have or do the things they want. "I can't travel to Italy because I don't speak Italian." "I can't finish college because I have to work." "I can't leave this job because I need the benefits."

People with **oomph** focus on what they **can** do and not their limitations. They use their **Oomph Power**, the "god within" of enthusiasm to reach their goals.

It's Easy to Recognize People with Oomph

I was fortunate to work almost twelve years as a special assistant to the Mayor of Louisville, Kentucky, Jerry Abramson. As Louisville's greatest cheerleader, Mayor Abramson earned the highest approval ratings in city history. I believe **Oomph** is the Mayor's middle name and I saw him exhibit all of the following **oomph** qualities:

☞ People with oomph are "above average."

People with **oomph** always do a little bit more, and that is a key secret to outrageous success. People with **oomph** never settle for just "getting the job done."

The salesperson who makes one extra call a day will earn more than other sales people who quit early. The student who studies an extra hour a day gets an extra fifteen days of learning each year.

The Success Motivation Institute calls it "the slight edge" concept. They say the person or organization that wins isn't 100 or even 10 times better than the competition. They're simply the ones who are a little better at or do a little more of the important things.

> The average person puts only 25 percent of their energy and ability into their work. The world takes off its hat to those who put in more than 50 percent of their capacity, and stands on its head for those few-and-far-between souls who devote 100 percent.
>
> *Andrew Carnegie*

People with **oomph** don't just coast through life doing just enough to *just* get by. They put their whole self into whatever they're doing and then they go the extra mile. People with **oomph** are not content with being "average" because average means you're as close to the bottom as you are to the top.

The Nike advertisement says: "Just do it." I believe if you want Outrageous Success, then don't "*Just* Do It." Do it with **oomph!**

☞ People with oomph are optimists

If you've got **oomph**, you expect more than others think is possible. You also risk more than others think is safe and dream more than others think is practical.

You think, "No matter how bad the economy is doing now, it's bound to improve." Optimism isn't wishful thinking or ignoring life's realities. It *is* choosing to focus on the positive, rather than the negative. Optimism is a conscious choice or selective perception.

Psychologist Martin Seligman, author of *Learned Optimism,* discovered the **oomph** power of optimism in the often discouraging profession of life insurance sales. His research showed that sales people who "saw the glass half-full" sold 37 percent more insurance than pessimists. Why? Because the optimists didn't believe a few poor sales days meant they wouldn't do better in the future. The optimist's motto is, "The more rejections I can take, the more sales I will make!"

Always borrow money from a pessimist. They don't expect to be paid back.

As CEO ("Chief Expert of **Oomph!**"), I was able to convince my husband to move to my dream house on the banks of the Ohio River. Most people don't want to live on the river because it's not a question of *if* the river will flood; it's a question of *when*. Where other people saw only muddy basements and power outages, I saw beautiful sunsets and river breezes. But I'm not a "blind optimist." Our first purchase was a set of matching hip wader boots!

☞ People with oomph make decisions and keep commitments

People with **oomph** do what they say they're going to do despite circumstances. They never say, "Sure, I'll try to do it, if nothing else comes up, if I don't get a better offer, and if I feel like it."

People who can't decide, can't succeed. People who say "I'll try..." are actually thinking, "I'll go through the motions, but I don't expect to succeed." They're already thinking up excuses to give up. People with **oomph** have more determination than excuses. They move forward with commitment instead of lagging behind with excuses.

William Hutchinson Murray wrote in *The Scottish Himalayan Expedition,* "Until one is committed there is hesitancy...The moment one definitely commits oneself, then providence moves too. All sorts of things occur to help one that would never otherwise have occurred."

☞ **People with oomph live in Technicolor**

There are two types of employees: Those who quit their jobs and leave, and those who quit their jobs and stay.

Peter Drucker

This description by management expert Peter Drucker is sadly accurate. Many people just go through the motions, collect the paycheck and go home. And many people live their entire lives in a gray zone.

I believe with **oomph**, it's like when Dorothy went from the black and white world of Kansas to the Technicolor world of Oz! **Oomph** gets you out of the gray zone and makes you more fully aware of the world around you. It doesn't mean you're loud, extraverted and hyped-up with high-octane enthusiasm for everything. **Oomph** just means being 100% *alive.*

Oomph means you live your life on purpose and not by accident!

I would rather have 30 minutes of wonderful than a lifetime of nothing special.

Shelby in the play Steel Magnolias

So, what's it going to be for you?

You can live in the gray zone or in **Technicolor**.

You can just go through the motions, or be fully **involved**.

You can focus on your limitations or always expect the **best**.

You can settle for mediocrity or strive for **more**.

You can "*Just* Do It." Or you can do it with **oomph** and enjoy **outrageous success**.

It's your choice!

Chapter Two

10 Ways to Re-Energize Your Attitude

I have read dozens of motivational books and heard many motivational speakers and their message is always the same:

"Just have a good positive attitude and your life will be great!"

Well, I have *had* a good, positive attitude my entire life, but my life hasn't <u>always</u> been great. I've certainly had my share of personal and professional challenges. So, I know that is just not true! Things *can* and **will** go wrong.

However, as speaker Larry Winget says, "Having a good positive attitude will help you **DEAL** with the things that go wrong in your life." So, as a motivational speaker myself, I don't tell my audiences, "**BE** positive." I tell them: "**STAY** positive and re-energize your attitude every single day."

Attitude is your perspective of life. Your perspective is determined by your thoughts and your thoughts are what you tell yourself each conscious moment of the day.

I'm so positive that I'd go after Moby Dick in a rowboat and take the tartar sauce with me. *Zig Ziglar*

The **most important tip of this book** is to:

Choose your own attitude and don't let anyone else choose it for you! *Susan Miller*

You can choose to be positive or you can choose to be negative. No one else can **force** you to be either one. Your attitude is *your* choice. Other people may attempt to control your circumstances, but they cannot control your attitude unless you let them. You and you alone are responsible for your attitude. You choose whether to be in a good mood or a bad mood. And you choose how other people affect your attitude.

I often hear from seminar attendees, "My boss (or spouse or co-worker or child) makes me so mad." And I answer, "If that person can **make** you mad, then they are choosing your attitude for you and they are driving your bus!"

A woman once told me, "My mother should be a travel agent for 'guilt trips' because she makes me feel so guilty." Again, I told her that no one can **make** you feel guilty. Don't let your mother drive your bus!

You either take responsibility for your life or you feel victimized by the world. The choice you make to either play the victim or to take personal responsibility will determine whose power grows—yours or someone else's.

> No one can make you feel inferior without your permission.
>
> *Eleanor Roosevelt*

But simply thinking and saying, "I'm going to be positive and have a great attitude" doesn't do it. You have to **work** at staying positive every day. It's not easy. You have to take deliberate action to have a positive attitude. You can't just think about being positive, you have to **act!**

Whatever your reality is today, this is just your starting point. The cards you are dealt in life are less important than the way you play them. Every day you're offered a new deal and new cards.

> The first step toward getting somewhere is to decide that you're not going to stay where you are.

Here are ten ways to re-energize your attitude for outrageous success:

#1 Weed your head of negative thoughts

To re-energize your attitude, you must learn to be aware of your thoughts and listen to what you tell yourself.

A man becomes what he thinks about all day long.

Ralph Waldo Emerson

Psychologists say we have over 40,000 thoughts a day and, unfortunately, 70% of those thoughts are negative!

How often do you catch yourself thinking:

"I hate this traffic."

"I look fat."

"I sounded like an idiot."

"These kids are driving me crazy."

"I hate this rainy weather."

Where do our negative thoughts come from? I believe they are planted in our subconscious mind when we're very young.

Business guru Brian Tracy says, "Your own level of self-acceptance is determined largely by how well you feel you are accepted by the important people in your life. Your attitude toward yourself is determined largely by the attitudes that you think other people have toward you. When you believe that other people think highly of you, your level of self-acceptance and self-esteem goes straight up."

The Low Self Esteem Group will meet Thursday at 7 pm. Please use the back door.

When I speak to audiences about attitude, I take a large plastic flowerpot, hold it on top of my head and say:

"I want you to pretend this flower pot is my head. If we fill it with soil and drop a seed in it and give it some water and sun, what happens? The seed will grow, right?

Your mind is like this flowerpot; whatever seed is planted in it will grow. And seeds are planted when we're young.

When your parents said, 'We love you. We're so proud of you. You can do ANYthing!' they were planting flower seeds.

When your teachers said, 'You are so smart. That's a beautiful picture. You always have great ideas,' those words were flower seeds.

When other kids said, 'Here's an invitation to my party. I want to sit next to you at lunch. We want you to be on our team,' those words were flower seeds.

And each of those seeds grew into a flower.

But many people didn't receive flower seeds when they were growing up. Their parents said, 'Wipe that stupid look off your face. Who do you think you are? Can't you get *anything* right?' Those words were weed seeds. And they grew into weeds.

Teachers also planted weed seeds when they said, 'Try to keep up with the others. Once again, you got it wrong! You're never going to amount to much.'

Other kids might have said, 'You're ugly. You dress funny. You can't sit at our table. You're too fat. You're too skinny. We don't want you on our team.'

Those were weed seeds. And weeds quickly choke or crowd-out the flowers. So those people who have had weed seeds planted, have flower pots filled with thriving nasty weeds instead of beautiful flowers."

DO THIS!

Write down what you heard growing up from:
Your parents: ______________________________
Your teachers: ______________________________
Your classmates: ______________________________

You must be careful about what you allow to enter your mind because your mind is like a garden. It will grow whatever is planted.

Earl Nightingale

What was planted in *you*r head when you were young? Weeds or flowers? And what seeds have you been planting yourself?

Well, if your flowerpot is full of weeds instead of flowers, I have some good news. You can WEED your flowerpot! Yank out the weeds and then plant your OWN flower seeds.

If you think, "I can't get that job," yank it out and replace it with this flower:

"I am smart and capable enough for that job."

If you think, "I shouldn't have done that; I really blew it," just yank that weed and say to yourself: "I forgive myself for being human and next time I'll do better."

Fill these lines with **positive** self-descriptive words:
I am ____

____

Remember: other people may have planted weed seeds in our young, fertile minds; but it is our responsibility now to weed our own flowerpots.

Don't blame your parents or teachers for what they did or didn't tell you. Realize they did the best they could with what they had and now it's up to you. Be totally accountable for your attitude.

#2 Go ahead...Make your day!

The difference between a good day and a bad day is the attitude you *choose* for that day. Each morning your thoughts decide what kind of day you're going to have.

When people ask me why I'm always so happy and full of **oomph**, I tell them I **CHOOSE** to be happy. It's a deliberate choice I make each day.

> I believe folks are about as happy as they make up their minds to be.
>
> *Abraham Lincoln*

Be careful of what you think about when you first awaken each morning because research shows that first half-hour is when your subconscious mind is at its most suggestible. Your brain waves are still in a relaxed alpha state so your thoughts are more powerful than later in the day when there are more distractions.

If you lie in bed after the alarm goes off and start thinking negative, self-defeating thoughts like, "I hate getting up. I don't feel like working today. I should have followed up with that client and I know I lost that sale. I'll probably be late again and the boss will be mad. I'm gonna have a lousy day, " what kind of a day will you have? That's right, a LOUSY one!

Instead of planting weed seeds, think **positive** thoughts when you first awaken and **positive** things will happen.

You can complain because roses have thorns, or you can rejoice because thorns have roses.

Ziggy

My Daily Attitude Re-Energizing Ritual:

Each morning, when the alarm goes off, and before I even lift my head from the pillow, the very first thing I do is SMILE—a really *big* SMILE.

I tell myself, "The first thing I did today is SMILE and the last thing I will do tonight is SMILE and no matter *what* happens today, I am going to choose to *stay* positive."

Next, I thank God for waking me up. I believe any day I wake up above ground is going to be a good one!

Then I do a Gratitude Inventory and think about all the blessings I have to be thankful for.

Next, I ask myself, "What great things are going to happen to me *today*?" I have found if I *expect* great things to happen, they usually do.

After I clearly visualize the wonderful day I **know** I am going to have, I throw back the covers, get up and make it happen.

Try my Attitude Re-Energizing Ritual tomorrow morning and jump-start *your* day.

This is the day the Lord has made. I will rejoice and be glad in it.

Psalm 118:24

#3 Think about what you <u>want</u>, not what you *don't* want

The subconscious mind does not accept the negative "don't" or "won't." It only concentrates on the rest of the message.

If I tell you, "*Don't* picture a rainbow over an elephant," what's the first thing you do? Right! You picture a rainbow over an elephant.

If you think, "I won't smoke today" or "I'm not afraid of snakes" or "I won't eat that gooey, pecan roll with the caramel icing..." you're just feeding your brain with those images.

Messages framed in the negative may communicate the opposite of what is intended. That's why lifeguards are trained to say, "Walk around the pool" instead of "Don't run!"

The "principle of dominant thought" says it is impossible to simultaneously be both optimistic and pessimistic. We are only capable of dealing with one thought at a time.

So, think only positive thoughts when you communicate with yourself. During your morning re-energizing ritual, instead of thinking, "I'm so busy, this is going to be a stressful day," say to yourself, "I have lots to accomplish today and I will be in control of my time and get done want needs to be done."

Instead of thinking, "I won't fall below my sales quota this month," say to yourself, "I will meet and exceed my sales quota this month."

Instead of thinking, "I don't want to be lonely," say to yourself: "I want a successful relationship."

These are positive affirmations and they work wonders.

We didn't lose the game; we just ran out of time.

Vince Lombardi

#4 Think of yourself as the person you want to be.

It is a psychological fact that whatever you want to accomplish must first be impressed upon your subconscious mind. Success is a state of mind. If you want to be successful, start thinking of yourself as *being* successful. If you want to be confident, tell yourself you **are** confident!

Have you ever thought, "I am such an idiot!"? Just the other day I left my hotel key in the room and caught myself thinking "Stupid Susan!" I immediately replaced that thought with, "Smart, sometimes-too-busy-to-remember-everything Susan" as I went to the front desk and requested another key.

During my daily Attitude Re-Energizing Ritual, I also think about a personality trait or quality I want to work on that day. I was once in Pittsburgh to present a seminar and while lying in bed I thought, "Today is going to be a great day and I will work on being more patient. I want patience."

I went down to the seminar room and when the first attendee walked up to the registration table, I said, "Hello, I'm Susan Miller," and she said, " Hello, I'm Patience." Her name was Patience O'Malley! I couldn't believe it. I told her, "I was just *thinking* about you!"

Controlling how you think about yourself can also get you through tough situations.

Rebecca Mark is a former Enron CEO who witnessed the Enron culture turn increasingly ruthless. She described in a *Vanity Fair* article about being in meetings with Enron officials who would criticize and condemn her for not producing enough profits. She endured the abuse by simply telling herself that she was the smartest person in the room. " I was looking at them but it wasn't real," she said. "It was like an out-of-body experience."

DO THIS!

- Take one or two minutes every day to see yourself as the person you want to be.
- Picture yourself as understanding, patient, kind or whatever you want to be, and hold that picture in your mind.
- Your mind will do its best to make your picture a reality.

#5 Tell yourself: "I CAN do this!"

I don't cook. Ever. My husband says, if we are what we eat, then I'm cheap, fast and easy! Each evening I tell him, "Honey, go forth. Hunt and gather and bring back food for me and the dog!"

I make lots of jokes about not cooking, but notice, I didn't say. "I CAN'T cook." I say, "I *don't* cook." "I choose NOT to cook."

I have eliminated the word "can't" from my vocabulary because:

Anything you tell yourself you *can't* do, you *won't* do.

It's absolutely true! If you think:

"I can't save money."

Guess what? You're right. You can't! And even if you *try* to do the thing you think you can't do, you won't succeed. And then you'll tell yourself, "I *knew* I couldn't do that." We never prove ourselves wrong. We only prove ourselves right.

My Negative Self-Talk used to be:

"I can't exercise because I'm on the road too much."

So I changed it to this Positive Self-Talk:

"I can exercise at least once a week while on the road and three times a week when I'm home."

If you catch yourself thinking, "I'll never get a raise," then immediately stop that negative thought and replace it with this positive affirmation, "I can and *will* ask for the raise I deserve!" Stop thinking and speaking in negatives.

> If you keep saying things are going to be bad, you have a good chance of being a prophet.
>
> *Isaac Bashevis Singer*

When you talk negatively about a situation, it always seems to grow worse. But the reverse is also true. Talking positively about a situation always seems to increase positive results.

I love the story about the two shoe salesmen who were in a remote corner of Africa. The first guy sends a telegram back to his office: "No prospect of sales. STOP. Natives don't wear shoes."

The other salesperson's letter read, "No one wears shoes! We can dominate the market! Send all available stock!"

If you think, talk, walk and act like a winner, you'll BECOME a winner.

DO THIS!

Write down one thing you tell yourself you can't do:
I CAN'T ______________________________

____

Next, write down the reasons why you *think* you can't do it:
I can't do this because: ______________________________

____

____

Next, think of one easy part that you CAN do and write it here:
"I CAN ______________________________

____

____

Always *think* of what you have to do as easy and it will become so.

Emile Coue'

#6 Choose really useful attitudes instead of really useless ones

Now that you know you are responsible for choosing your own attitude, then what **kind** of attitude should you choose? Nicholas Boothman, in his book *How To Make People Like You* says when interacting with another person, you should choose a really **useful** attitude like one of the following:

Really *useful* attitudes: kind, confident, curious, patient, relaxed, interested, supportive, helpful, engaging, obliging, humorous

---

These are attitudes that create rapport and cooperation and will serve you best in almost any encounter.

The opposite is true, too. You will rarely receive cooperation if you exhibit really **useless** attitudes such as:

Really *useless* attitudes: anger, sarcasm, rudeness, blame, pessimism, boredom, condescension, impatience, suspicion, self-pity, negativity

---

In any difficult situation, ask yourself, "What do I want to accomplish right now and which attitude will serve me best?"

I was once flying home to Louisville from Charleston, SC and when I arrived at the airport, I was told all flights through Atlanta had been cancelled because the airport had been closed due to a breach in security. Many people were yelling at Troy, the poor gate agent, but when it was my turn, I chose really useful attitudes. I was sympathetic ("Having a rough day?"), curious ("Can you get me home?") and appreciative ("Thank you so much!") when Troy gave me a hotel and meal vouchers and even some chocolate-chip cookies homemade by his mother!

He who angers you conquers you.

Elizabeth Kenny

#7 Tell yourself, "I'm having a GREAT day!"

My friend Susan Stanley needed to get to a hotel in upstate Michigan to present a seminar. Bad weather made her miss her flight connection, so she drove six hours, arrived at the hotel at 4:30 am, and had to get up at 5:30 am. At the end of the eight- hour seminar, when she told the audience she had had only one hour sleep the previous night, everyone wanted to know, "How did you get through the day? You were so energetic." She told them she repeated to herself all day, "I am energized. I am full of energy. I am having a GREAT day!" As long as she was saying that to herself, it was true. Once the audience left, *then* she collapsed!

The next time you have one of "those days" when nothing goes right, try saying to yourself, "I'm having a GREAT day!"

The only person you have to convince is yourself.

> Motivation is like a bath.
> It doesn't last very long so you need to take one every day.

#8 Don't let people take up space inside your head without paying you rent.

Does this sound familiar? You lie in bed, unable to sleep, and think to yourself, "When she said that to me, I should have said this." Or, "When he did that to me, I should have done this." That other person is the last person you think about before you finally fall asleep and the first person on your mind when you wake up.

And you know what the other person is doing while you're lying there worrying about them? That's right. They're fast asleep!

We waste way too much **oomph** worrying about what other people think about us, when the fact is, they're not thinking about us at all!

I tell my audiences, "When I was a teacher in my 20's, I worried, 'What do the other teachers and students *think* about me?' When I was in my 30's and 40's and working in city government, I worried, 'What do the other employees *think* about me?' Now that I'm in my 50's, I realize **no one** was ***ever*** thinking about me!"

Since having that valuable revelation, when a gate agent at the airport asks if I have any excess baggage, I can now answer, "Not anymore!"

DO THIS!

- Identify WHO is taking up space inside your head:
- Ask yourself: "Do I benefit in any way when I think about them?" If the answer is "no," switch your thoughts to something or someone else.
- You will notice an immediate increase of **oomph**.

#9 See problems as "Creative Challenges."

Instead of dreading problems in your life, assume that something good is hidden within each problem and view it as a challenge.

> Whenever God wants to give us a gift, he wraps it up in a problem.
>
> *Dr. Norman Vincent Peale*

In other words: the bigger the gift you have coming, the bigger the problem you will receive. But if you look for the gift, you will always find it.

With any problem, stop and ask yourself, "What valuable lesson am I learning right now? What will I do differently if I encounter a similar experience?"

Then begin to focus on finding solutions. The instant you begin focusing on solutions, you use your **oomph** in a constructive way. Problems are inherently negative and solutions are inherently positive. Don't waste your **oomph** with finger pointing and guilt. Look to the future and think about and visualize the ideal solution to your challenge. Remember:

- **There is usually more than one right answer to any problem.**
- **You do not need to solve problems alone. Ask others for their input.**
- **Break your problem into pieces and handle one piece at a time.**
- **Always approach your problems with an attitude of confidence, not fear.**
- **Tell yourself, "Everything is happening perfectly."**

Karate students are taught that people are vulnerable when they fear being hit. Once you know you can take a punch, you have a huge advantage. Once you know you can handle any problem or adversity, when you realize that you cannot control **what** happens in your life; but you <u>can</u> choose how you *deal* with what happens, you give yourself enormous power.

We can't control what happens to us. But we can choose how we respond to it.

Victor Frankl, concentration camp survivor

#10 Keep it in perspective

For almost three years in a former life, I owned a helium balloon business. When I first started the business, I would often get upset with delays while delivering the balloon bouquets, until I learned to put things in perspective. "Relax," I would remind myself. "You're delivering *balloons*, not babies!"

We all have day-to-day hassles and little emergencies. What's important is to keep problems in perspective, and don't sweat the small stuff (and, as author Richard Carlson reminds us, it's *all* small stuff!)

Most people major in minor things.

Jim Rohn

When you feel stressed out, look beyond the moment and ask yourself, "Will this matter ten years from now, or even ten *minutes* from now?" Focus on the big picture and not the petty details. Ask yourself, "Does it *really* matter?"

And the next time you experience a problem, say this simple four-letter word to yourself: **NEXT**. Mark Victor

Hansen, co-author of the *Chicken Soup* books, believes this word has great power and should be used to handle all rejections. When you suffer a setback, ask, "What do I do **NEXT**?" This moves you farther down the road, away from the moment, and into the "big picture."

10 Ways to Re-Energize Your Attitude

1. **Weed your head of negative thoughts.**
2. **Go ahead...Make your day!**
3. **Think about what you *want*, not what you don't want.**
4. **Think of yourself as the person you want to be.**
5. **Tell yourself, "I CAN do this!"**
6. **Choose really useful attitudes instead of really useless ones.**
7. **Tell yourself, "I'm having a GREAT day!"**
8. **Don't let people take up space inside your head without paying you rent.**
9. **See problems as "Creative Challenges."**
10. **Keep it in perspective.**

Chapter Three

How to Set Goals for Outrageous Success

As I said in Chapter One, success means reaching your goals.

That's it! That's the true definition of success. Success simply means you get what you want. And what YOU want is different from what other people want. If you ask ten different people what they want in their lives, you will get ten different answers.

That's why success does <u>not</u> mean having all the money in the world; unless you say, "I WANT all the money in the world." Then that is YOUR goal and reaching that goal is how YOU define success.

Too often, we let other people define success for us. Whenever you hear comments like "You *should* get a college degree," "You *should* have children," or "You *should* make more money," what you're hearing are **other** people's definitions of success.

If the should doesn't fit, don't wear it!

If success means, "reaching your goals," then to create your own definition of success, you need to create a **map** of your personal, physical and professional goals.

Just like you wouldn't go on a long road trip without a road map, you can't reach your goals without a detailed, *written* map. It's not a map set in stone with no alternate routes. You don't have to know **how** you're going to get there and you get to adjust your route as you go. The important thing is to know **where** it is you **want** to go!

> You've got to be very careful if you don't know where you're going, because you might not get there.
>
> *Yogi Berra*

One of the most common questions I am asked is, "Why do I have to write down my goals?" The answer is simple: when you write down your goals you are convincing yourself that you can achieve them. Writing down your goals brings what you want into sharp focus. Focus is what turns a vague sense of wanting *something* into a clear vision. It's like when I adjust the focus knob on my binoculars and a fuzzy red patch in the tree becomes a beautiful cardinal.

You must be able to visualize or see yourself succeeding at your goal. The clearer the picture you have, the greater the chances of making it happen. *See* yourself riding in your new boat, spending more time with your kids or arranging furniture in your new office.

Write down your goals and post them where you can see them –the mirror, refrigerator, dashboard of your car-so you will be constantly reminded about what you want to own, who you want to become or where you want to be.

If you aim at nothing, you'll probably hit it.

The best goals begin with these two words: "I Want." Not "I should," not "I wish," not "I think I'd like…" Simply: I WANT!

For OUTRAGEOUS SUCCESS, write down goals that have an end result that you really, *REALLY* want. In other words, dream BIG! The best "I want" is something you can't get out of your mind. It's an obsession.

Success is not the result of spontaneous combustion. You must set yourself on fire.

Reggie Leach

I have found when I do goal setting exercises in my seminars, many people have a hard time writing down what they want. They're too focused on why they **can't** do, be, nor have the things they want. As adults, we let time, money, education, background, and our environment act as limitations on our thinking. So, I suggest you think like a kid again while you write your goals. Have you noticed how children never set limitations on themselves? They really believe they can have, be or do *any*thing they want.

> Whatever the mind can conceive and believe, it can achieve.
>
> *Napolean Hill*

It's important the goals you write down are specific and measurable. For your Personal Goals, don't just say, "I want to be happy." You can't measure happiness. Instead, ask yourself, "What would *make* me happy—and why?" What do I want to own? Where do I want to go?"

When you set Professional Goals, ask yourself, "How much do I want to work? How much money do I want to make?" Don't just say, "I want to make more money" because "more" means nothing. Be specific! For instance: "I want to earn $______." "I want to finish my college degree." "I want to start my own business." "I want to retire at age _______ with $_______ a month income."

> If one advances confidently in the direction of his own dreams, and endeavors to live the life which he has imagined, he will meet with a success unexpected in common hours.
>
> *Henry David Thoreau*

When you set Physical Goals, don't just say, "I want to be healthy" (can you measure health?) Instead, say: "I want to lose ______pounds" or "I want to quit smoking," "I want to get this much more sleep each night," or "I want to lower my cholesterol level by this many points."

Six months before my 50th birthday, I wrote, "I want to lose 25 pounds before my birthday." So I paid $175 for a six-month membership to "Fitness on Frankfort," a work-out studio in our neighborhood. Six months later I had not lost a single pound. Apparently.... you have to show up! It's true. I paid $175 and then I **never** went back!

Goal setting is important, but goal *doing* is even more important! So, after you set your goal you must have an action plan to turn that goal into a reality. Know what you WANT and what you are WILLING to **do** to get it. I have lost 25 pounds in the past two years because I say, "I **will** walk 30 minutes or go to yoga class every other day." And then I *do* it.

I quit smoking by using the patch.
I put six of them over my mouth.

Steven Wright

DO THIS!

Step 1.

Write down what you really, *REALLY* want, and be very, VERY specific!

PERSONAL GOALS:
I want ______________________________

PHYSICAL GOALS:
I want ______________________________

PROFESSIONAL GOALS:
I want ______________________________

Step 2.

Identify the specific benefits for each goal: List all the reasons WHY you want to achieve each goal. What are the benefits for YOU? By asking yourself why **you** want these goals, you weed out any goals you set to please other people: "It'll please my father if I become a lawyer." Or, "My husband says I should lose weight." Avoid setting goals that only impress or satisfy *other* people.

Personal Goal Benefits: ______________________

____

Physical Goal Benefits: ______________________

____

Professional Goal Benefits: ______________________________

____

Step 3.

Identify the obstacles to reaching each goal: List everything that could possibly prevent you from reaching each goal: (ie: time or financial constraints.)

____

____

Obstacles are those frightful things you see when you take your eyes off the goal. *Hannah Moore*

Step 4.

Identify a support team:
List the people and/or resources that can help you overcome these obstacles.

____

____

Step 5.

Create an "I WILL" action plan:
Big goals begin with small steps. Now that you've identified your goals, you must create an **action plan** of the things you WILL do. Goals without an action plan are merely dreams.

Even if you're on the right track, you will get run over if you just sit there.

Will Rogers

Your action plan states what you are WILLING to do or WILLING to give up in order to get what you WANT. Anyone can dream. But to have outrageous success, you have to know what you are willing to do or give up to get it! When I wanted to lose 25 pounds, I was willing to give up mayonnaise and butter; but I was <u>not</u> willing to give up almond M&M's! So, I just eat fewer of them.

How to be successful:

1. Make a decision about what you want in your life.
2. Make a decision about what you're willing to give up to get it.

H.L. Hunt

To create your **Action Plan**:

- Visualize the end result and write your goal as though it is already accomplished. For example, "I live in a three bedroom house with a creekstone fireplace and a beautiful flower garden."
- Set a deadline for your goal. "I am driving my new

Mercedes on New Year's Eve, 2_____." "I am running in this year's Boston Marathon." "Today's date is _______ and I am wearing size______ pants."

A goal is a dream with a deadline.

- Identify all the steps between where you are now and the end result.
- Pick the EASIEST step and write down that you **will** take that step within the next 72 hours. Why 72 hours? Because you'll need the first two days to feel scared, nervous and rebellious. You are forming new habits and the old habits are still seductive.
- By the third day, get going! The first two letters of the word GOAL are GO.

Take the first, easiest step, celebrate that success and keep going.

Bad habits are like a comfortable bed, easy to get into, but hard to get out of.

Action Plan Example:

GOAL:

Today's date is ___________ and I live in my brand new three-bedroom house with a fenced back yard.

Benefits:

- I can use the money that I've been spending on rent

- Home ownership provides tax benefits
- I can get a dog!

Obstacles:
I don't have enough money for a down payment.

Support Team:
My sister-in-law is a mortgage banker.

Action Step:
Within the next three days, I will make an appointment to open a separate savings account at her bank and ask her how I can save for a down payment.

Most people spend more time planning Christmas and New Year's than their own lives.

Denis Waitley

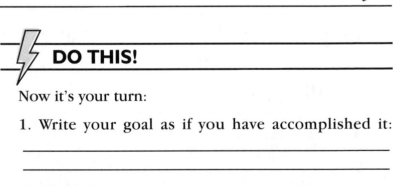

DO THIS!

Now it's your turn:

1. Write your goal as if you have accomplished it:

____

____

____

____

2. Write down the first action step you will take in the next 72 hours: ____________________

____

The first step is always the hardest, but once you get started, momentum will keep you going.

Good intentions are like crying babies in church. They should be carried out immediately.

Mark Twain

Step 6.

Believe you can do it!

To achieve any goal, you must believe you are going to be successful. If you don't believe in yourself and your abilities, you are likely to fail.

In one of my favorite songs, R. Kelly sings: "I <u>believe</u> I can fly." He doesn't sing, "I <u>think</u> I can fly," "I'll <u>try</u> to fly" or "<u>Maybe</u> I'll fly." He sings, "I **believe** I can fly!" You've got to **believe** it to **achieve** it!

The weakest words in the English language are: "I'll try."

The strongest words are: "I will!"

There is no *try*. There is only *do*.

Yoda in The Empire Strikes Back

Dr. David J. Schwartz in *The Magic of Thinking Success* says, "When you think, 'I will,' your mind performs two amazing acts: First, it shows you how to achieve your dreams and, second, thinking 'I will' supplies the energy you need."

In other words, if you think, "I will buy my dream house," the source of financing will appear. If you think, "I will get a job promotion," what you must do to make that a reality will become evident.

Today is a day for firm decisions. Or is it?

Step 7.

Review your goals daily

Make reviewing your goals part of your daily routine. Each morning, read your goals out loud as if you have already accomplished them. "I'm driving my new blue Lexus to my new job and I am smoke-free."

At night, before you go to bed, repeat the process to get your subconscious and conscious mind working toward your goals.

Every time you make a decision during the day, ask yourself this question, "Does this decision take me closer to, or further from my goal?" If the answer is "closer to my goal," then you've made the right decision.

Step 8.

Re-visit your goals and make adjustments if necessary

I frequently travel to Australia for seminars and speaking engagements. Each time the plane leaves the Los Angeles airport, it heads west. Then, during the sixteen-hour flight, the pilots will make thousands of minute adjustments based on wind currents, storms and other climatic changes. Closer to Sydney, the plane will finally zero in on an exact landing pattern and complete the trip.

The same principle is at work with our goals. When we first chart them, we know the destination, but we can and *will* change how we get there many times before we complete the trip.

If you say, "I WILL walk 5 days a week," and then you realize your schedule won't allow that large of a commitment, then change it to: "I WILL walk 4 days!"

If we set our goals too high and do not make adjustments, we only set ourselves up for frustration and failure.

So, visualize yourself living the life *you* want to live, turn those dreams into written goals, create your action plan, commit to it and you *will* enjoy outrageous success!

How to Set Goals for Outrageous Success

Step one. Write down what you really, REALLY want.

Step two. Identify the specific benefits for each goal.

Step three. Identify the obstacles to reaching each goal.

Step four. Identify a support team.

Step five. Create an "I WILL" action plan.

- Visualize the end result.
- Set a deadline for your goal.
- Identify all the steps between where you are now and the end result.
- Pick the EASIEST step and write down that you will take that step within 72 hours.
- By the third day, get going!

Step six: Believe you can do it!

Step seven: Review your goals daily.

Step eight: Re-visit your goals and make adjustments if necessary.

Chapter Four

Your "Oomph Bank" and Eight Awful Oomph Bank Busters

Does your employer or family think you have a bottomless well of energy—of **oomph**? Do they believe you just go to that well and draw out all the **oomph** you need to meet *their* needs?

The reality is, instead of a bottomless well, we each only have a small piggy bank of **oomph**. And we need to budget our **oomph** the same way we budget our money.

I was twelve years old when I first understood the concept of banks and budgets. I saved my babysitting money in an amber glass piggy bank and learned:

1. The more money I put in that bank, the more money I'd have to spend on movies and make-up.
2. If I empty the bank for these purchases, I may not have any money for "big ticket" items like a new miniskirt (this was the 1960's!)

I believe our **oomph**– our energy and enthusiasm- is as precious as our money and we must create a reserve of **oomph** so we have it when we need it. Just like we "save for a rainy day," it's important to have enough **oomph** socked away, ready to help us get through any rough times that come our way.

There are three basic types of energy:

1. **Physical energy** is the raw energy required for physical labor.
2. **Emotional energy** is required to feel love, happiness and joy.
3. **Mental energy** is the energy of creativity, problem solving and decision-making.

Business expert Brian Tracy believes most people fail to realize their potential in life because they burn up their energy at the emotional or physical level; therefore, they have very little energy left over for mental activities. I call it an over-drawn **Oomph** Bank account!

An over-drawn Oomph Bank account will result in burnout and stress.

Burnout is physical and emotional exhaustion caused by excessive demands on our emotional and/or physical energy. Stress simply means feeling out of control. Think about the last time you were stressed. Maybe you were stuck in traffic, your baby wouldn't stop crying or your boss ordered you to work late. Did you feel like the situation was out of your control?

Stress is a physical response to a perceived threat. As many as 1500 separate, documented physical changes occur in the human body in response to stress.

When you waste your energy getting upset over things you *can't* control, you deplete your **Oomph** Bank and become vulnerable to the physiological effects of stress.

In order to protect the limited amount of **oomph** in your **Oomph** Bank, you need to figure out what *causes* you stress so you can prevent problems from happening in the first place. Here are Eight Awful **Oomph** Busters. Which ones can you relate to?

#1 Self-Doubt

The only barrier between you and outrageous success is not something that exists in the real world. The only barrier is doubt about yourself and your abilities.

If you tell yourself you can, you can. And if you tell yourself you can't, you're right! *Mary Kay Ash*

And you will never prove yourself wrong. *Susan Miller*

Anything you tell yourself you **can't** do, you **won't** do. If you tell yourself:

"I can't ask that person out for coffee."
"I can't finish this job on time."
"I can't quit smoking."
"I can't remember names."
"I can't leave this dead-end job."
"I can't leave this unhealthy relationship."
"I can't ask for a raise."
"I can't lose 20 pounds."
"I can't go on a blind date."

Well, guess what? You're right!

You **won't** ask for the raise, you **won't** lose weight and you **won't** meet new people.

We never prove ourselves wrong. We only prove ourselves right!

If you think, "I'm too shy with new people," then that becomes your reality.

If you think:

"I'm not confident."

"I am so stressed out."

"I'm a lousy parent."

"I'm terrible at math."

"I'm no good at sales."

"I never know what to say."

"I'm **just** a _________________ (fill-in-the-blank)"

Then, so you are!

We become what we think about most of the time.

My audiences are surprised when I tell them I am sometimes plagued by self-doubts. As a motivational speaker, they believe I must *always* be full of self-confidence. However, like the saying, "Physician, heal thyself," I sometimes need a dose of my *own* medicine.

When I first began professional speaking, I spoke to a group of insurance agents and because they didn't laugh at all of my funny stories, I left the stage really doubting my abilities and myself. I seriously thought about taking my career in a different direction.

That same day I was introduced to a friend of a friend. When I told her I was a professional speaker, she proceeded to tell me about an amazing speaker she had heard over a year ago. As she described the "best speaker she had ever heard," it sounded like she was describing another local speaker, which just made me feel worse than I already did. But as she began re-telling her favorite story from the speech, I realized she was talking about ME! Wow! I told her, "Thanks! I **needed** that!"

That moment rescued me from my earlier self-doubt and now I try to recapture that moment whenever any self-doubt threatens to bust my **oomph.**

DO THIS!

What are your self-doubts? Write them here:

____

____

____

Why do you think you have these doubts?

____

____

____

What is some positive feedback you've received that can counter these doubts?

____

____

____

#2 Making excuses and blaming others

What was the first thing you did as a child when you did something wrong and were afraid of the consequences? Right! You made excuses or looked for someone to blame:

"He started it!"

"My *friends* said we should ignore the No Trespassing sign!"

"I got a failing grade because the teacher doesn't like me."

And the most famous excuse of all, "The dog ate my homework!"

Many of us have used excuses throughout our lives to explain everything from being late ("I was stuck in traffic") to forgetting important dates ("I had a 'senior' moment") to severe business or personal problems ("I only drink to help me get to sleep.")

We also blame others for our shortcomings or unhappiness:

"My spouse is a jerk."

"My boss takes advantage of me."

"My mother embarrasses me."

"She made me lose my temper."

When you blame others or events, you give away your power to that person or event. You make them the "villain" and yourself the "victim." Have you ever noticed how victims begin every sentence with "**if?**"

"**If** it weren't for traffic, I'd be on time."

"**If** I didn't have to take care of these kids, I'd make more money."

"**If** my boss would give me better assignments I could get a promotion."

Instead of blaming others or making excuses, take 100% personal responsibility for everything that happens in your life. This means "Be proactive," the first habit in *7 Habits of Highly Effective People* by Steven Covey. Dr. Covey believes that any time you think a personal problem is caused by events or others, that *thought* is the problem.

When you miss the target, never in history has it been the target's fault.

Dr. Gerald D. Bell of the University of North Carolina states, "You are 100% responsible for your own happiness. Other people are not responsible. Your parents aren't responsible. Your spouse isn't. You are. So, if you're not happy, it's up to you to change something. It's not up to someone else to 'fix it' for you."

Blaming circumstances like your parents, your background, your spouse, your health, your job, the company, the school system, the economy, the government, the *weather*...solves nothing. Blame won't fix anything and it prevents you from taking responsibility for creating the life you want.

People are always blaming their circumstances for what they are. I don't believe in circumstances. The people who get on in this world are the people who get up and look for the circumstances they want, and, if they can't find them, they make them!

George Bernard Shaw

#3 Negative People

We all know people who brighten a room just by walking into it. And you also probably know someone who brightens a room just by walking OUT of it!

Be careful of Negative People—people who were weaned on lemons—because they'll bankrupt your **oomph** bank.

How do you feel when someone with a bad cold sneezes in your face? YUCK! Well, that's what happens when you're in direct contact with a negative person. Negative People are infectious and they will infect YOU if you let them.

When a co-worker constantly complains ("I hate this job. I hate my husband. I hate this doughnut."), they want you to feel as lousy as they do. Don't go to their Pity Party!

Remember:

Negative people are NOT interested in solutions to their problems. They are only interested in finding fault with everything around them.

You are only wasting your precious **oomph** when you say, "Hey, cheer up! Things can't be that bad." As Jerry Seinfeld points out, "Misery loves company. Look at a fly-strip. If a stuck fly sees another fly coming, he never says, 'Go around!' "

Negative people want you to be as miserable as they are and accept a life of boredom and mediocrity. If you tell them your dreams or goals, they'll shower you with killer phrases like, "Don't waste your time," or "It'll never happen."

Coach Rick Pitino in *Success is a Choice* calls negative people the "Fellowship of the Miserable." Pitino says, "Negative people usually surrender during adversity. They look for reasons why things won't work, rather than explore why they *will* work."

Great spirits have always encountered violent opposition from mediocre minds.

Albert Einstein

When I tell my seminar participants they need to stay away from negative "poison people," someone invariably asks, "But, I have to *sit* next to a negative person at work. How do I get away from *them*?" To that concern I respond, "You may not get to choose who you sit next to at work, but you **do** get to choose who you talk to during your breaks. You **do** get to choose who you go to lunch with. So, CHOOSE to stay away from the negative people."

If the negative person is your boss, you either need to develop a set of blinders to stay focused on the positive aspects of your job, or get another boss! (See Chapter Ten: "Eight More Strategies to Re-Energize Your Job"). This may sound like a drastic measure, but your boss is the greatest influence on your job success and happiness.

What if the negative person is a family member or a close friend? Since you can't totally eliminate them from your life, arrange things so you only have to deal with them in small doses. Try not to be alone with the negative person and, if possible, communicate by e-mail rather than in person or on the telephone.

DO THIS!

Identify the negative people in your life:

____

How much time do you spend around them?

____

How can you minimize the time you spend with them?

____

____

People will try to rain on your parade because they have no parade of their own.

#4 Resentment

When I complain to my husband of wrongdoings, real or imagined, that I have "suffered," he listens patiently because he understands the value of venting. But if I bring it up again a day, month or year later, he'll quote the infamous Budweiser commercial, "Let it go, Louie; let it go!" My husband is a wise man!

Resentment is like carrying a sack of potatoes all day. It takes too much of your valuable **oomph**. Slowly but surely, you will be ground down by fatigue caused by worrying about what someone did or didn't do.

You cannot shake hands with a clenched fist.

Indira Gandhi

Either drop that heavy sack of hurt and resentment, or choose to tell the other person how you feel. If you decide to confront the person, you may want to use the Assertive FeedBack Technique created by my friend and fellow trainer Susan Stanley.

DO THIS!

Fill-in this outline, practice until you can recite it in your sleep and follow it exactly when you confront the other person:

1. I am ______________________________ .

(Write one word ONLY! You can say "angry," or "upset"; but not "pissed-off"—that's two words!)

2. When I am/see/hear ______________________ .

(Specify their behavior *without* saying the word "you" or "your.")

3. What I want/need/prefer: __________________
____ .

(Give the specific solution and it's okay to use "you" or "your" here.)

Here's a script one of my seminar attendees developed to say to her boss:

"I am embarrassed (1)

When I am yelled at in front of the other staff. (2)

What I would prefer is that you would talk to me privately and calmly if there is a problem." (3)

Note that she was very specific about the boss's behavior and did not make the mistake of saying, "I am embarrassed when you treat me disrespectfully." He wouldn't know what she was talking about! She also didn't say "I am embarrassed when **you** yelled at me." He would only hear the word "you" and become defensive.

Once you've said your piece, just say "thank you" and leave! Don't dilute the message with nervous babbling. And if the other person says, "What are you talking about?" Just take a deep breath, and repeat what you just said. Some people need to hear it twice!

> Never be bullied into silence. Never allow yourself to be made a victim. Accept no one's definition of your life; define yourself.
>
> *Harvey Fierstein*

#5 Killer Phrases

Advertising executive Charles Bower once said, "An idea is delicate. It can be killed by a sneer or a yawn; it can be stabbed to death by a quip and worried to death by a frown on the right man's brow."

Have you ever suggested a new idea and then had it smashed, broken or discarded by someone saying the following:

- "We tried that before and it didn't work"
- "You've got to be kidding"
- "No one will like it"

- "It's not in the budget"
- "Don't rock the boat"
- "Put it in writing"
- "If it ain't broke, don't fix it"
- "We've always done it *this* way"

These are what author Charles "Chic" Thompson in his book *What a Great Idea!* calls "killer phrases" and they're also huge **oomph** busters.

The one who says it can't be done should never interrupt the one who is doing it.

I once heard Thompson speak at a conference and he suggested we each compile a list of the killer phrases we hear in our own workplaces and get others to contribute to the list. Then make it against company rules to use any of those phrases at work, especially when trying to generate new ideas in a brainstorming session.

Brilliant ideas are those that were first thought to be wrong, but later shown to be obvious.

DO THIS!

Make a list of the killer phrases you hear at work *or* at home. ______________________________

____

____

____

Make a poster entitled "These Killer Phrases are NOT Allowed" in this Home/Office"

Be aware of how these killer phrases bust your **oomph,** stifle creativity and take the wind right out of everyone's sails.

#6 Procrastination

Are you a procrastinator? I know, you want to wait a few minutes before you answer! I used to wait until the last minute to do anything and would justify my procrastination by thinking, "Pressure creates diamonds!"

It took me almost five years to finish this book. Why? Three words: "Paralysis by analysis!"

Never put off 'til tomorrow what you can do the day after tomorrow. *Mark Twain*

Does this sound familiar? You talk about what you're going to do; you plan it, analyze it and prepare for it, but you never actually DO it!

"Some day I will..."

"I'm still working on...."

"I can't until..."

You can't build a reputation on what you're GOING to do.

Henry Ford

Of course planning is important. But starting is even *more* important. If you're always putting off what needs to be done, people stop relying on you and soon, they start overlooking you. Procrastination is not only an **oomph** buster, it's also a **trust** buster.

And if you snooze, you lose. As Jack Foster points out in *How to Get Ideas*, "Otto Titzling invented the brassiere but never took out a patent on it. Phillipe de Brassiere did."

Warning! Dates in calendar are closer than they appear!

According to the book *Procrastination and Task Avoidance* by Joseph Ferrari, we postpone what needs to be done for one of three reasons:

- We like the thrill of time pressure

- We're unable to choose, or
- We fear failure and would rather be seen as lazy than imperfect.

And I would add one more reason to this list:

- We don't *like* to do it

Whatever the reason, I call it a Procrastination Complex and have found the following cures to be helpful:

☞ Strive for accomplishment instead of perfection

If you strive for perfection, you will never see results.

☞ Decide to spend just a short time on a task you've been avoiding.

When there's something I don't want to do, I force myself to spend five minutes on the task. No matter how big or unpleasant it is, (like balancing the dreaded checkbook) I can spend five minutes on it. I usually don't even notice when five minutes have passed and I'm still working.

☞ Tell people your deadlines.

I told hundreds of people when I thought this book would be published, so I had to finish it or lose their trust! Another interesting phenomenon is that the more people you tell about what you want to achieve, the more they want to help you reach your goal.

☞ Burn your boats

When Julius Caesar invaded a foreign country, he would burn the boats so his army knew retreat was impossible. It was either win or die. No alternatives, no excuses. Think about all the excuses *you* create that keep you from what you need to do. Don't give yourself and your unfinished tasks an escape route. Burn your boats.

DO THIS!

Something I've been procrastinating about is:

____

____

I haven't started because: ______________________

____

One small task I **can** complete within 3 days is:

____

____

Now put that item on your daily To-Do list and do it!

#7 Clutter

☞ Does your bedroom closet have a Ph.D? That means "piled higher and deeper!"

☞ **Have you ever walked into your office and felt tired just *looking* at all that stuff?** That's your body's reaction to information overload.

☞ **Do you waste an hour a day looking for stuff that's "lost" in your office or closet?**

Well, if you don't love it, and/or you don't use it, it's clutter. Clutter includes the magazines you're going to read "some day," the too-small clothes you hope to fit into again, the stuffed file folders and half-finished crafts projects.

Clutter at work and at home is a huge **oomph** buster.

The 5000 year-old Chinese art of Feng Shui identifies clutter as the greatest enemy of "chi" or energy. Feng Shui teaches that if energy can flow easily through a room, your life will be more harmonious and happy—and clutter is an obstacle to reaching this relaxed and calm state.

When my husband and I moved last year, instead of moving boxes of stuff from one basement to another basement, we ruthlessly de-cluttered our lives by bringing into our new house only things that passed this test:

> Have nothing in your house that you do not know to be useful or believe to be beautiful.
>
> *William Morris*

We took bags of still-useful items and wearable clothes to two different women and children's shelters and took appliances that needed repairs and other "yard sale stuff" to the Goodwill. What a burst of **oomph** that created!

You've got too much stuff if... people come to your door and want to buy things from your yard sale and you're not having one.

Jeff Foxworthy

Clutter is simply postponed decisions. Career counselor Barbara Sher believes clutter isn't a problem; clutter *solves* the problem of commitment. We keep all this stuff around that keeps us from actually doing the things we really need to do. "Oh, one of these days I'll organize these catalogues/clothes/magazines/ broken appliances/ project materials." Phone calls you need to return, correspondence that awaits your reply and the supply room that needs restocking, are the clutter of uncompleted tasks.

One of these days is none of these days.

Big Al Juodikis

DO THIS!

- **Toss ten things from most rooms in your house.** The bathroom is an especially fertile place to try this (dried-up toothpaste, out-dated vitamins, etc.) as is the kitchen, basement or garage. Put useable items in bags and take to a shelter or the Goodwill. Many organizations will even pick them up.

- **Don't succumb to De-Cluttering Remorse.** That's when you go through the bags and start pulling out things because you "may" need them again or you "may" hold a yard sale. Trust me: you won't!

- **Keep only the items on your desk that relate to your current project.** Don't use your desk as a storage area; it's a work space. Clean it off at the end of each day so you can start again fresh tomorrow.

- **Before you buy something, ask yourself, "Is this something I really need? Or is it just something I *want*?** And if I just want it, do I really love it and will I *still* love it a year from now?"

> Is there not more to life than getting stuff? And then getting more of it, bigger of it, faster of it and then stuffing what you can't use now somewhere so you can use it later?
>
> *Richard Stine*

#8 Your Achilles' Heel

As I admitted in the introduction, I am an extremely impatient person. I believe "instant gratification" takes too long and I pace in front of the microwave. So when someone is not able to immediately answer my question, get what I need or do what I ask, I tend to get impatient, annoyed or even angry.

Impatience is my Achilles' heel. You may remember from the story in Greek mythology that when Achilles was born, his mother, Thetis, tried to make him immortal by dipping him in the river Styx. As she immersed him, she held him by one heel and the place where she held him remained untouched by the magic water and that part stayed mortal and vulnerable.

I have several "weak points," but impatience is truly my Achilles' heel and it has cost me valuable **oomph**. I also know that awareness of a problem is the first step on the road to recovery. So now, when restaurant service is too slow, traffic is stopped or I find myself in the longest line at the grocery store, instead of showing my impatience, I tell myself, "Take a Chill-Pill, Susan and relax!" I then force myself to take two calming breaths and think about something pleasant. I find this works *almost* every time.

DO THIS!

My Achilles' Heel or hot button is ____________________

____

When my button is pushed I usually react by:

____

____

Instead, I will ________________________________

____

Eight Awful Oomph Busters

1. **Self-doubt**
2. **Making excuses and blaming others**
3. **Negative people**
4. **Resentment**
5. **Killer phrases**
6. **Procrastination**
7. **Clutter**
8. **Your Achilles' Heel**

Chapter Five

The 10 Best Boosters for Emotional Oomph

Emotional **oomph** is the energy that is necessary to feel love, happiness and joy.

Maximize your energy and enthusiasm by practicing these 10 emotional **oomph** boosters.

#1 Surround yourself with Positive "Can-Do" People

I have discovered there are two types of people in the world:

"Rise and Shiners" and "Rise and Whiners."

When the alarm goes off, Rise and Whiners gripe:

"Yuck, I *have* to go to work today."

The Rise and Shiners say:

"Thank goodness I *have* a job!"

The Rise and Whiners will consume your time, energy, and effort if you let them. It is in your best interest to avoid them and hang out instead with Positive People who inspire, validate and bring out the best in you.

We become like the people we associate with every day.

If you associate with people who hold Pity Parties to complain about their mediocre lives and misfortune, you will soon become one of them yourself.

If you tell Rise and Whiners your dreams, they'll laugh and ridicule you. They would rather you fail than succeed because your successes make them feel uncomfortable about their own failures. If you fail, they feel better about themselves.

But if you tell positive, successful people your dreams, they'll say, "Sounds great. How can I help?" Positive People encourage you when you need it. Positive People know there is plenty of success for everyone. Positive People want you to win.

The best thing about surrounding yourself with Positive People is that you start "feeding" off each other's **oomph** power. Problems are solved, ideas are created and opportunities are recognized.

Surround yourself with positive people and the benefits will rub off on you. *Rick Pitino*

DO THIS!

Write the names of the Positive People who inspire and validate you: ______________________________

____

____

Make a goal to spend more time with these people.

Example: I will call/e-mail __________ by this date and time ________________ and suggest we get together by ____________________________ .

#2 "Stay on your mat."

> **Don't bother just to be better than your contemporaries or predecessors. Try to be better than yourself.** *William Faulkner*

When I started practicing yoga last year, I would look around at these human pretzels bending their bodies into incredible shapes while I could not even touch my toes. I figured they must be looking at me and thinking, "She can't even do this simple position."

I busted my **oomph** comparing myself to others until I learned this wonderful lesson from my yoga teacher Paul

Long: "Stay on your mat." In other words, don't look at what anyone else around me is doing on *their* mat. Don't worry about where they are in their yoga journey. I need to keep my focus on what I am doing on *my* mat.

I still look at the flexible people around me at yoga, but instead of comparing myself to them, I get **inspired** by them and I just keep doing the best I can.

> When you are content to simply be yourself and don't compare or compete, everybody will respect you.
>
> *Lao-Tzu*

DO THIS!

Who is someone to whom you've compared yourself?

____

What does this person specifically do or have that you wish *you* could do or have? ______________________________

____

How does this person inspire you? ______________________________

____

____

#3 Thank God!

It doesn't matter what your religious beliefs are, we all need help and guidance and we need to cultivate an "attitude of gratitude."

I always thank God for waking me up each day, and I go to church on Sundays to thank God for my blessings. This "attitude of gratitude" means I don't take all the wonderful things in my life for granted. I believe my blessings come from God and don't just "happen."

> i thank YOU God for most this amazing day; for the leaping greenly spirit of trees and a blue true dream of sky; and for everything which is natural which is infinite which is yes.
>
> *e.e. cummings*

More than 300 studies show that people who believe in something greater than themselves are better able to weather life's storms.

Fellow speaker David Eastman says, "Gratitude is your way of accepting love from the universe. Whatever you're grateful for, the universe will send more of it your way." What a cool concept! David suggests creating a "Gratitude Inventory."

DO THIS!

1. List 10 **people** in your life—in addition to your family—that you're thankful for. Include people you haven't met yet, but who have influenced your life in some way, like authors, artists, speakers, etc.
   1. ____________________
   2. ____________________
   3. ____________________
   4. ____________________
   5. ____________________
   6. ____________________
   7. ____________________
   8. ____________________
   9. ____________________
   10. ____________________

2. Next, create a list of 10 **places** you really appreciate. These places can be as general or as specific as you like. Maui, the public library, your erogenous zones — it's all up to you!
   1. ____________________
   2. ____________________
   3. ____________________
   4. ____________________
   5. ____________________
   6. ____________________
   7. ____________________
   8. ____________________
   9. ____________________
   10. ____________________

3. Now, create a list of 10 **items** or possessions you're grateful for:
   1. ______________________________
   2. ______________________________
   3. ______________________________
   4. ______________________________
   5. ______________________________
   6. ______________________________
   7. ______________________________
   8. ______________________________
   9. ______________________________
   10. ______________________________

Just creating a Gratitude Inventory will boost your **oomph** and you can use this list when you thank God for your blessings!

You can also find spiritual **oomph** and inner peace on-line at www.dailyzen.com, which posts a Zen quote each day. Send your e-mail address to www.deeshan.com to receive daily or weekly meditation tips.

#4 Do something...ANY thing for someone you don't know (and who can't repay you)

I get a great **oomph** boost each time I give the fast-food employee at the counter or drive-through window a $5 or $10 bill as a tip (and I'm a fast-food junkie so I do this often!) These aren't "charitable donations" I can deduct from my taxes; but the smiles I get back are more valuable than a tax break.

The important part of this **Oomph** Booster is to have **no** expectation of being repaid. That's the very nature of giving. If you expect something in return, you're not giving. You're just exchanging.

What do we live for if not to make the world less difficult for each other? *George Eliot*

Here are some examples of other things you can do with no expectation of return.

Identify a local homeless shelter and:

- Call your local pizza parlor, give them your credit card number and order pizzas delivered to the shelter. (Call the shelter first and see how many people are there that night so you're sure to order enough pizza for everybody.)
- Whenever you bring a new article of clothing/furniture/appliance/book into your home, put an old article into a box and regularly take the box to the shelter.
- When you travel, save hotel soaps, shampoo and coffee packs to donate to the shelter.
- Buy twin-sized blankets and sheets for the shelter bunk beds.
- Take your old magazines to the shelter or a retirement home or hospital.

The true value of an individual is how he treats a person who can do him absolutely no good. *Ann Landers*

#5 Lighten up!

When I think back on some of the most stressful moments in my life, I now realize I could have improved many of those moments if I had just lightened up.

I was called the "Minister of Fun" in my former job as the City of Louisville's special events director; yet, I often took *myself* way too seriously. Now I know the key is to take my **job** seriously and **myself** lightly!

I was presenting an all-day communications seminar to a group of about 50 people in Milwaukee. Toward the end of the day, I was tired of standing so I sat down in the middle of the banquet table that held the overhead projector. With no warning, the table broke down the middle and I fell to the floor, along with the projector and my 16oz. mug of tea. I was so surprised that I just sat there for a few seconds, and then I started to laugh! I laughed so hard tears ran down my face. After I managed to pick myself up, I announced to the class, "I guess I really **do** need to start my diet!"

When you can find the humor in a situation, you defuse much of its negative power ove you and its drain on your **oomph** bank. And laughter is like "natural Prozac." It releases the feel-good internal chemicals called endorphins that give you a sense of well being. So seek out any opportunity to have a good laugh.

You grow up the day you have the first real laugh at yourself.

Ethel Barrymore

DO THIS!

1. Describe a recent stressful situation you experienced:

2. What is the one funny thing you can now find in that situation? (Look really hard!)

3. Collect short jokes and cartoons. Here are some of my favorites:

- "I spilled spot remover on my dog. He's gone now." *Steven Wright*
- There are two Rules for Success: Number one. Never tell everything you know. Number two.
- I have a clear conscience because I have a bad memory.
- 42.7% of statistics are made up on the spot.

4. Sign up at www.the-mouth.com and receive daily one-liners from late night comedians.

Life is too important to be taken seriously. *Oscar Wilde*

#6 Ask for what you want

I stay in lots of hotels and I almost always enjoy a free breakfast. Why? Because I **ask** for it! I first ask for a free breakfast coupon, and I usually get one.

If the front desk clerk says they don't have any coupons, then I ask (always very nicely) for a free upgrade to the "Presidential Suite." That always gets a laugh at the front desk of standard hotels like the Holiday Inn, but the clerk often gives me a Jacuzzi room or a kitchen suite with refrigerator.

If you don't ask, you probably won't get it. Don't expect to get something because you want it, earned it, need it or deserve it. People cannot read your mind.

If you want your co-worker to stop making loud phone calls, then say, "I am distracted when I hear loud phone calls; could you please lower your voice?" There. Now that wasn't so hard, was it?

If you want a raise or promotion, ask for it. Rarely does a boss say, "You've been working so hard. Here's a big raise and promotion." So **you** need to say, "I have drafted a memo that outlines the problems I have solved and the money I have saved the company the past twelve months. I also did some research (see www.salary.com) and found the average salary for this job is 15% more than my current compensation. I am requesting a salary increase of $__________."

Assertiveness means asking for what you want and not *assuming* the other person knows what you want. "Assume" means you didn't ask or didn't try.

Now, you may get a "no," but don't let that discourage you. You're still better off than before because you've planted a seed for future discussions. Sales people know that over 60% of all buying decisions are made after the customer has said "no" four times. So, when you get a "no," keep asking.

> Ask a little, get a little. Ask a lot, get a lot. *Larry Winget*

#7 Climb out of your comfort zone

> Unless you walk out into the unknown, the odds of making a profound difference in your life are pretty low. *Tom Peters*

Each of us has a comfort zone where we feel sheltered and safe. The activities and situations in our comfort zone are familiar and non-threatening. They are things we do easily, like speaking to friends or co-workers or completing routine job tasks.

However, we all occasionally face experiences or challenges that are *outside* our comfort zone. Challenges such as leaving a long-time relationship, getting a new job, or the knee-shaking challenge of public speaking!

Your comfort zone is different from mine or anyone else's. You may be paralyzed with fear if asked to speak in front of a large group, whereas I've made a career out of public speaking. (My mother says, "I can't believe you get paid to speak. Your father and I used to pay you to be quiet!")

But we all have the same two fears that keep us inside our comfort zones: Fear of Failure ("I can't ask for a promotion because I couldn't handle the job") and Fear of Rejection ("I can't leave this unhealthy relationship because no one else will want me and I don't want to be alone.")

Most people would rather be certain they're miserable, than risk being happy. *Robert Anthony*

Climbing out of your comfort zone is the only way to get unstuck and move forward, but it does take courage. There is a saying, "Most people are not risk averse—but loss averse." In other words, we spend too much time looking at all the dangers that may happen if we climb out of our comfort zone. But, the more you climb upward, (and the less time you spend looking down!), the stronger you get. You will be building up your emotional muscles over time. And just like with all muscle growth, you will always feel some pain before you see growth.

Fear stops action. Action stops fear. *Margaret Bourke-White*

I left the comfort zone of a great job with city government after almost twelve years because I felt 'root-bound" and needed to get re-potted in order to grow. It took three years of just *thinking* about starting my own business before I had enough nerve to leave. The first year without a steady paycheck was scary, uncomfortable and... *exhilarating*. Now, after six years of owning my own speaking and training business and traveling over 100 days a year, I have created a new comfort zone and can't imagine ever working again in a traditional office job.

You don't need to *leap* out of a comfort zone. Just taking a few exploratory steps is a great **oomph** booster.

A ship in port is safe, but that is not what ships are made for.

DO THIS!

Complete these sentences:

The Comfort Zone I would like to step out of is:

____

____

I stay in this Comfort Zone because: ________________

____

____

Three small steps I could take are: ________________

____

____

I will take step one by: __________________________

____

#8 Make an effort to spend more time with family and friends

Friendships multiply Joys and divide Griefs. *Thomas Fuller*

Fast Company magazine recently reported in a cover story that over fifty million Americans work full or part-time at home. Not only do more of us work in isolation, we communicate through e-mail and the Internet, making it even easier to be physically out of touch. This is why it's more important than ever to make people a priority and create ways to connect with others.

Spending time with our family and friends requires effort and planning, but the results are always worth it.

Happiness is having a large, loving, caring, close-knit family in another city. *George Burns*

I don't have children of my own, but I am blessed with a fabulous stepdaughter and two-year-old granddaughter. After a few hours' visit with them, my batteries are recharged and I'm definitely re-energized. Because they live out of town, I know that I need to make more of an effort to see them.

It's the same with friends. Sometimes I find myself "cocooning" in my house after an extended speaking engagement and going days or weeks without seeing my friends. I have found if I don't have regularly scheduled get-togethers, then I have to make the effort to see other people. It's not enough to wait for friends to seek *me* out.

> Friends are those rare people who ask how we are and then wait to hear the answer. *Ed Cunningham*

DO THIS!

Write down the names of people whose company you enjoy, but you haven't seen lately.

____

____

____

Pick one person from your list and invite them to meet for coffee, lunch, or an after-work drink. They will be happy to hear from you!

#9 No worries

One of the best expressions I learned from the wonderful Australian people I have met during my speaking trips down under is "No worries!" If you ask an Aussie for anything, they respond, "No worries!" Worry is an **oomph** buster, so having "no worries" is a great **oomph** booster.

Do you have lots of worries or "what if's" in your life? "What if I lose my job? What if I get mugged? What if I get sick?" "What if's" create unnecessary anxiety in your life. Anxiety means worrying about the future. Counter anxiety with this positive thought, "No matter *what* happens, I can handle it."

Guilt means worrying about the past. "I **should** have done this" and "I **should** have done that." No matter how hard you try, you cannot change the past nor control the future; so, don't worry! Stay in the **present**.

> I am an old man and have known a great many troubles, but none of them ever happened. *Mark Twain*

DO THIS!

Make two columns:

Worries I can **DO something** about	Worries I can do **nothing** about:
• Credit card debt	• The weather
• ________________	• ________________
• ________________	• ________________
• ________________	• ________________
• ________________	• ________________
• ________________	• ________________
• ________________	• ________________

List every worry you have in the appropriate column.

Accept the problems you can't control and look for solutions to the ones you can.

#10 Smile!

Some wise person once said, "If you're not using your smile, you're like a man with a million dollars and no check-book." I agree!

A smile gives you instant **oomph** and it's the easiest way I know to:

☞ **Attract other people to you**

☞ **Go from a rotten mood to a good one**

☞ **Improve your appearance**

☞ **Fake it 'til you can make it**

Now I'm not saying you should walk around with a big grin on your face that makes you look like you've got the IQ of celery! I'm talking about a smile that starts with your mouth and ends with your eyes.

How does a smile help you "fake it 'til you can make it?" Remember this:

People believe what they **see**, not what you **say**.

Let's say your boss has asked you to make a report at a big meeting and, like most people, you are scared to death of public speaking. If you get up in front of the audience with either a frown or a deer-caught-in-the-headlights look on your face and say, "I'm so **happy** to be here!" nobody will believe you!

However, if you stand up straight, **smile** and then begin your remarks, everyone in the audience will believe you're full of confidence. And, amazingly, you will begin to feel more confident.

A smile attracts people to you because people go toward the sun!

Dave Eggleston is the executive director of a large marketing association and I've never seen him frown. He immediately puts new members at ease and established members enjoy his great sense of humor.

As a marketing expert, Dave knows that people like to buy from friendly people. Friendly people wear a smile. Therefore, in order to sell more, you must be perceived as friendly, and to be perceived as friendly, you need to smile. It's simple logic that works.

A man without a smile should not open a shop. *Chinese proverb*

But, have you ever thought, "I just don't **feel** like smiling"? Smile <u>anyway</u>! Neurologists have documented how the "action" of the mere twitch of a smile can set off the "**re**action" of a stream of happy endorphins through the body. It seems the smile forces certain facial muscles to contract, which decreases the flow of blood in nearby vessels, which cools the blood which lowers the temperature of the brain stem which then produces more serotonin which puts you in a perkier mood—wow!

So it's virtually impossible to smile **and** stay in a lousy mood and that's why a smile is instant **oomph.** And smiles are reciprocal. If you smile at another person there's an almost 100% chance that person will smile back. So smile anyway and always be the *first* to smile.

The 10 Best **Oomph** Boosters for Emotional **Oomph**

1. **Surround yourself with positive "can-do" people.**
2. **"Stay on your mat."**
3. **Thank God.**
4. **Do something...ANY thing for someone you don't know (and who can't repay you).**
5. **Lighten up!**
6. **Ask for what you want.**
7. **Step out of your comfort zone.**
8. **Make an effort to spend more time with family and friends.**
9. **No worries.**
10. **Smile!**

Chapter Six

Seven Super Boosters for Physical Oomph

You can't have **Oomph Power** if you're tired, thirsty, out-of-shape or flat-out hungry.

You can't have **Oomph Power** if you don't replenish your power *source.*

You can't have **Oomph Power** if you usually spend your time eating Cheetos, drinking soda pop, getting three hours of sleep at night and the most exercise you get is bending over to pick up the remote control.

Here are seven, simple, super easy ways to boost your physical **oomph.**

#1 Break your fast

Did you have a healthy breakfast this morning? Probably not. Research shows that 60% of Americans skip breakfast. And breakfast decides whether or not your day will be filled with **oomph** or oomph-less.

As I mentioned in Chapter Two, I don't cook. I am cooking-impaired and use the smoke alarm as a timer. The only thing I know how to make for dinner are reservations.

> Cooking takes too much time. You have to plan the menu, buy the food, prepare and serve, wash the dishes and then six months later, start all over again! *Joan Rivers*

However, I *do* eat a healthy breakfast every single morning. Nutritional experts all agree: breakfast is the single most important meal of the day. Breakfast is the gas that fills your energy tank. If the tank is empty, you're not going to go very far when you press the gas pedal. Going without breakfast sends your body into semi-starvation mode and it's hard to make up the missed nutrients.

Eating breakfast boosts your **oomph** and your memory. A study by the University of Wales found that students who skipped breakfast scored 22% lower on a word-recall test. Why? Breakfast boosts blood sugar needed to make acetylcholine, an important memory neurotransmitter.

An elaborate breakfast is not necessary for these benefits. Just make sure you eat something high in protein and high in carbohydrates, like peanut butter on whole-wheat toast, preferably within a half-hour of getting up.

It's important to control the blood sugar boost and raise it slowly and steadily rather than in a spike. The carbohydrates in toast will give your body a quick burst of energy to get you moving. The protein in the peanut butter is digested more slowly than the carbs and provides a steady stream of energy to keep you alert and productive until it's time for a healthy mid-morning snack.

Every morning I eat a bowl of Kashi GoLean Crunch!® cereal, which can be found in the health food section of most grocery stores. And I eat it with non-fat chocolate milk! You may think, "yuck" instead of "yummy," but don't knock it 'til you try it. The fiber in the cereal fills me up and the chocolate milk feeds my chocolate addiction.

If a bowl of healthy cocoa puffs isn't *your* ideal breakfast, you can find some easy breakfast recipes at www.mayohealth.org.

DO THIS!

Complete the following:

For breakfast this morning, I had: ____________________

____

Tomorrow morning I will eat this for breakfast:

____

____

I've been taking Flintstones vitamins. I don't feel any better, but I can stop the car with my feet.

#2 Have a snack attack

Forget about eating three big meals a day. Instead, after your healthy breakfast, continue to eat something every two to four hours throughout the day to maintain your blood sugar at an optimal level.

Oomph is energy and energy comes from glucose, which is sugar in its simplest form. The food we eat gets converted into glucose, which is the brain's primary energy source.

Eating foods that contain protein will boost alertness and concentration by increasing tyrosine, the revitalizing amino acid in the brain.

And eating small snacks throughout the day helps prevent weight gain because your body gets the message there's no need to store fat against famine.

Pick healthy snacks like a carton of fat-free yogurt, a power bar (I'm partial to Clif Luna Bars®) or an apple and peanut butter crackers.

DO THIS!

To keep your metabolism up and your blood sugar from dropping, eat these five "meals' every day:

- Small breakfast
- Healthy mid-morning snack
- Small lunch
- Healthy mid-afternoon snack
- Small dinner
- Healthy evening snack

#3 Go and get a tall glass of water

I mean right now! Put this book down and go get a tall glass of water. Don't worry about what *kind* of water (mineral water? carbonated water?) Good old tap water will do just fine.

Now drink the water whenever you feel like it. When the glass is empty, go fill it up and repeat the process. That's all you need to do to add more re-energizing water to your life.

If you prefer cold water, keep sports bottles in the refrigerator. I drink hot decaffeinated green tea all day from my plastic, sixteen ounce "mega-mug." I keep the mug on my desk and take it along on every business and vacation trip.

Water flushes out toxins and helps your body absorb nutrients. If you're thirsty, you're already slightly dehydrated and your body is already two percent low on water. According to Susan Kleiner, Ph.D. and author of *Power Eating*, losing just one to two percent of your body weight in fluid can lower mental and physical performance by up to twenty percent.

DO THIS!

- Drink at least six 8-ounce glasses of water a day.
- Drink water **before** you get thirsty.
- Drink water **before** you exercise.
- Switch to a larger glass.
- Add some **oomph** to plain old water by adding a small amount of orange or lemon juice.
- For every caffeinated beverage you drink, drink 8 ounces of water along with it.

#4 Get more Zzzzzzzzzz's

Research shows that lack of sleep does two things:

1. It shortens your life.
2. It makes you stupid.

That may sound harsh, but it's true. A lack of sleep depletes the immune defense system—which speeds aging—and it has a pervasive effect on brain function. It's during REM (rapid eye movement) that our brains create new neural circuits and lack of sleep "short-circuits" this process.

A lack of sleep also affects our mood and self-confidence. A University of Pennsylvania study showed that when subjects were limited to four and a half hours of sleep for one week, they felt more stressed out and depressed than the subjects who had eight hours.

So sleep is *not* a luxury; it is a necessity. Sleep is *not* a waste of time; it serves a valuable purpose. A National Sleep Foundation survey found the average American gets only six hours and twenty-three minutes of sleep. The amount of sleep each one of us needs is personal; yet, experts believe no one should get **less** than six and a half-hours and few need more than nine hours.

How much sleep do *you* get? Are you getting *enough* sleep?

If you recognize any of these signs, you may be sleep-deprived:

☞ **You fall asleep at your desk in the afternoon.**

☞ **You can't stay awake after dinner.**

☞ **You need four alarm clocks to wake-up.**

☞ **You fall asleep while driving** (an estimated 100,000 car crashes annually are blamed on sleepy drivers).

☞ **You have frequent insomnia.**

DO THIS!

☞ Go to bed half an hour earlier each night this week.

☞ Check-out www.sleepfoundation.org

Try these proven insomnia cures:

- No chocolate after 2:00 pm and no caffeine at *any* time.
- No alcohol after 6:00 pm; it will keep you in the lighter sleep stages rather than in the deeper, more restful stages.
- Don't go to bed unless you feel you can fall asleep.
- Sleep on your side to promote easier breathing and reduce snoring.
- Cover the clock so you're not reminded how long you've been awake.
- Go to bed and wake up at the same time every day, even on weekends.

#5 Move it!

Just like my "I don't cook" jokes, I used to also repeat jokes about not having a regular exercise program:

- I don't exercise because if God wanted us to touch our toes, He would have put them on our knees!
- I have a favorite machine at the gym; it's the vending machine.
- Whenever the urge to exercise comes upon me, I lie down a while and it passes.
- I don't like to jog...it makes the ice jump out of my drink.
- I like long walks...especially when they're taken by people who annoy me.

My cooking jokes are harmless because I can find ways to eat without cooking myself. But, I realized I can't get someone else to exercise for me and lack of exercise *is* harmful to my health.

The Surgeon General has said exercise is as important as quitting smoking for a long, healthy life. Exercise wakes up the nervous system, speeds up the metabolism, increases blood flow to the brain and is an instant **oomph** booster.

But it's the classic catch-22: I know I need to **move** to get more energy, but I don't have the **energy** to move!

Fortunately, it isn't necessary to run a marathon or exercise until you fall over gasping for breath to get the benefits.

A study by Northern Arizona University found that a ten-minute brisk walk is sufficient to boost your **oomph**. The key is to work hard enough to break a sweat and do it regularly. I walk or practice yoga four days a week when I'm home and run through airports and lift my luggage into overhead bins to get my exercise on the road!

My mother says she likes to ride her bicycle on the beach. What *really* happens is mom gets on her stationary bicycle she placed in the largest of her home's two bathtubs. She turns on the fan and gazes at a beach picture over the tub as she pedals away!

DO THIS!

Try these easy ways to add some movement to your normal routine.

- Park at the rear of shopping center parking lots.
- Take the stairs instead of the elevator.
- Lift small weights while talking on the phone.
- Shake your head from side to side when offered dessert!

#6 Don't hold your breath

My friend Paula Kommor uses the following exercise in her fabulous stress management classes. She tells everyone to make a tight fist and hold it for fifteen seconds. Then she asks, "How many of you were holding your breath during that time?" Everyone realizes that's exactly what he or she was doing! Paula uses the exercise to illustrate that when we feel stressed or angry, one of the first things we do is stop breathing! And that is when we need to breathe the most.

It is incredible what such a simple act as breathing can do for the mind and body. Research shows that proper breathing can:

☞ **Cut stress levels in half.**

☞ **Lower blood pressure.**

☞ **Help you think more clearly.** A University of Illinois study showed that although the brain accounts for only 2 percent of body weight, it uses 20 percent of glucose and 25 percent of all the oxygen you consume. More oxygen means better brain cells!

☞ **Help you lose weight.** High doses of oxygen kick-start your body cells into burning stored fat for energy.

But to get all these benefits, you must breath **correctly.** Take a deep breath right now.

Did your chest move? If so, you're breathing **in**correctly. It's the abdomen that should expand each time you inhale.

The lungs are your secondary respirators. The diaphragm (a pancake-shaped muscle under your ribcage) is your primary respirator. When you take a "belly breath," the diaphragm drops down allowing the lungs to fill completely with oxygen and the abdomen protrudes.

Shallow chest breaths only fill the top of the lungs, straining them and sending the body into its "fight or flight" response. Shallow breathing also doesn't sufficiently rid the body of carbon dioxide. A buildup of CO_2 has a toxic effect on the body and makes you feel sluggish.

Although our lungs can hold two gallons of oxygen, shallow breathing draws only two pints of oxygen. That means most people only get 20-25 percent of the oxygen our lungs were designed to hold.

The goal is to take deep, slow, controlled breaths through the nose to get more oxygen into the lungs and, subsequently, into the bloodstream.

The beauty of belly breathing is, no one has to know you're doing it! It can be your own private weapon against stress and anxiety.

How to Belly-Breathe:

- ☞ **Straighten your back, relax your shoulders and close your mouth.**
- ☞ **Slowly inhale through your nose to the count of four. Pretend you're blowing up a balloon in your belly.**
- ☞ **Let the breath rise through your ribs and up to your shoulders.**
- ☞ **Hold the breath for four counts.**
- ☞ **Exhale, like a sigh, to the count of eight.**

DO THIS!

- Put BREATHE! cards around your office, home or on the dashboard of your car to remind you to do it!
- Practice your belly breathing while waiting for your computer to boot up, when someone on the telephone puts you on hold or while you're stuck in traffic.
- When stressed, try the yogic art of one-nostril breathing: Cover your right nostril with your thumb and slowly inhale and exhale through your *left* nostril several times to calm yourself.
- If you want instant **oomph**, try the same one-nostril breathing through your *right* nostril.

#7 Take time for yourself every day

I can only please
one person per day.
Today is not your day.
Tomorrow doesn't look
good either.

Do you ever sit down to read the newspaper and think, "Okay, I'm going to relax now;" but the little voice in your head begins listing all the things you <u>should</u> be doing right then, like mowing the grass, washing the dishes or something "productive?"

Jim Temme, in *Productivity Power,* says that always thinking about what you *should* be doing is the Puritan work ethic taken to the extreme. Work is important but learning to relax is *just* as important. The whole purpose of physical relaxation is to allow yourself to recharge your emotional and mental batteries.

Most people fill-up their Daily To-Do lists and forget to include themselves. Administrative assistants at my seminars tell me how their supervisors will often make them work through lunch, stay late to finish paperwork, and then call them at home with more directions! At the same time, the "admin" is also trying to take care of the kids, the spouse and help out friends and other family members.

Remember what you are told whenever you fly: "Put your own oxygen mask on *first*."

To boost your **oomph**, block out thirty minutes of commitment-free time on your schedule. Do this every single day. Use this time any way you wish: watch Wheel of Fortune, take a power walk, read junk mail or give yourself permission to do absolutely nothing.

And learn to say "no" to some things so you can say "yes" to others. When someone asks you to be on another committee or take care of his or her kids for the umpteenth time, don't automatically say, "I'll be glad to." As First Lady Nancy Reagan advised, "Just say NO!"

Seven Super Boosters for Physical Oomph

1. **Break your fast.**
2. **Have a snack attack.**
3. **Go and get a tall glass of water.**
4. **Get more Zzzzzzz's.**
5. **Move it!**
6. **Don't hold your breath.**
7. **Take time for yourself every day.**

Chapter Seven

Emergency Oomph Boosters

Have you noticed how you never get a warning before you're attacked by a case of the blahs? You can be having a great day, and then all of a sudden, the blahs hit and you just don't want to do *anything*. I call it "getting stuck."

I have discovered there are different degrees of feeling stuck:

- Basic Blahs (also known as Common Complacency)
- Major Misery
- Lasting Lethargy

Emergency Oomph Boosters for Handling the Basic Blahs

When you find yourself stuck with Basic Blahs, follow these steps:

1. Immediately put some upbeat music on the CD or tape player and turn up the volume.

2. Drink a cup of tea or coffee (but only if you can tolerate caffeine).

3. Dance for ten minutes to the music, or, even better:

4. Put the upbeat tape or CD in your Walkman, go outside and take a fast walk.

5. When you return home, do one or more of the following:

   - Take a bath ("Calgon®, take me away!") or brisk shower.
   - Read a motivational book (like ***Oomph Power***!)
   - Telephone your most positive friend or family member and ask them for a pep talk. Be careful not to do this *too* often or they'll change their phone number!
   - Rent or go watch a funny movie or just tune your TV to Comedy Central. Studies by the American Association for Therapeutic Humor show that laughter increases endorphins, body hormones that act as natural mood elevators.
   - Think of something nice you can do for someone else and *do* it! Get outside your own situation and focus on someone *else*'s problems.

The best way to cheer yourself up is to try to cheer somebody else up. *Mark Twain*

Managing Major Misery

If you have been divorced like I have, then you may have also experienced Major Misery. I have read many books about the emotional impact of divorce, and one statement that really resonated is:

It's better to *be* alone than to *wish* you were.

Major Misery can be triggered by any kind of loss. And the hardest but most important **Oomph** Booster is to take action when you feel your worst. When you're experiencing major misery is *precisely* when you need to take action.

There's a principle in physics that says a body in motion tends to stay in motion. If you will do something, *anything*, to get moving, it becomes easier to keep going.

Don't just do something. Stand there. *Rochelle Myer*

Five years ago, my father suffered a heart attack and, for about eight hours, was in a coma before he died. He and my mother were out of town at the time and so all five of us children could only wait helplessly by our telephones before Mom called and said that Daddy was gone.

That was the most horrible day of my life and I spent it on my knees cleaning out my kitchen cabinets. I wasn't aware of what I was doing; I just got down on the floor and started on the drawer with the most accumulated junk. That's how I dealt with my Major Misery.

Dr. Michael Crabtree, professor of psychology at Washington & Jefferson College says any task that requires repetitive movement like vacuuming, grouting bathroom tile or ironing is a type of "chore therapy." The rhythm puts you in a state of "passive attention" so you stay focused on your task and not on your misery.

So, take action when you feel your worst, even if it's just vacuuming the living room carpet!

When you find yourself in a hole, stop digging. *Will Rogers*

Emergency Oomph Boosters for Lasting Lethargy

Sometimes problems with your love life or work life can cause Lasting Lethargy. Maybe a personal relationship ended, you were passed over for a promotion or you experienced some other type of loss. It's important to recognize the loss you experienced, declare a fixed time to grieve and give yourself permission to mourn or feel disappointed.

If you find the blahs lasting more than a week, follow these steps:

1. Make an appointment to see your doctor.
2. Set a kitchen timer or alarm clock for 60 minutes. (Note: do not exceed one hour!)

3. Now, really wallow in your miserableness. Put on your rattiest bathrobe or sweat pants, find something chocolate or salty, crunchy or sweet (or all of the above) to eat. Do NOT drink alcoholic beverages at this time!
4. Get in bed or lie on the sofa and watch some mindless TV. You are too vulnerable to watch Home Shopping Network right now so stick to "The Price is Right," "Wheel of Fortune" or ESPN. "Jeopardy" may be too much of a strain for you right now.
5. It's okay to acknowledge how miserable you feel and "cocoon" for an hour or so. But the entire time, remind yourself, "This too shall pass."
6. When the alarm goes off, immediately put on your upbeat music and do your best to follow the steps above for Basic Blahs.
7. Be sure to get out and socialize with someone. Even though this is probably the last thing you want to do right now, *force* yourself to call a friend and meet for coffee, a movie, a walk, a talk—anything to get out and change your atmosphere.
8. Follow the Goal-Setting steps in Chapter 3 to figure out what you really want and take a small achievable "action step" toward that goal.

Again, if you find your lethargy lasts more than a week or two, see your doctor to determine if your lethargy is a symptom of depression. It has been estimated that one in four women and one in eight men will suffer an episode of depression sometime in their lives. It can be a great relief to know there is a valid reason for your blahs and there are many options for treatment.

In a recent study of depressed people, researchers at Duke University found that more than half of those who jogged or walked for half an hour, three times a week, overcame their depression without the use of antidepressants.

Am I really happy or is it the Prozac®? *Seen on a T-Shirt*

Dig Your Well Before You're Thirsty

Because we are rarely given fair warning before an attack of the blahs, it's important to have these blah-busting **oomph** boosters on hand for when you need them:

- The work, home, and cell phone numbers of your best "cheerleader" friends.
- A Victory List of your accomplishments. Add to this list whenever you set a personal, physical or professional goal and achieve it.
- Chocolate
- A few of your favorite funny videos. Steve Martin's *The Jerk* can always chase away my blues.
- This book with your favorite quotes highlighted in bright colors.
- An "**oomph** tape/CD." A study dubbed "The Mozart Effect" determined that music *can* affect your mood. So make a personal compilation of the music that always gets you going. When you hear a great song

on the radio, make a note of the title and artist; find it on-line and for a small charge, you can download it to your **oomph** CD.

And always remember:

- You are not alone. EVERY person you know has his or her own problems.
- In two days, tomorrow will be yesterday!

Chapter Eight

A Dozen Ways to Re-Energize Your Relationships

My favorite Barbra Streisand song says it best, "People who need people are the luckiest people in the world." Having people to talk with, share successes and failures, to vent frustrations and to love, laugh and cry with is the purpose of life.

We all need people and **oomph** attracts people to us. **Oomph** is defined in the *Random House Dictionary* as "1. Energy, enthusiasm, vitality and 2. **Sex appeal**." It's true! People *are* attracted to people with **Oomph.**

How we *relate* to the people in our lives is the key to outrageous success. Here are a dozen ways to help re-energize your personal and professional relationships.

#1 When you meet someone, ask yourself, "How can I *help* this person?"

To dramatically improve all of your relationships, remember this universal rule: you have to ***give*** in order to ***get***. Any good relationship, whether it be at home or on the job, is built on a foundation of loving and giving.

When you meet someone, *don't* ask yourself, "What

can **they** do for me?" Ask instead, "What can **I** do for them?" Always think in terms of what the other person needs, especially if you attend a "networking" event.

Networking is *not* about collecting a pocketful of business cards. It is about making links from people *you* know to people *they* know and expecting nothing in return.

Each time you meet someone new, look for ways to help or support that person. Don't think, "What's in it for me?" or "Now you owe me." Help others without keeping score because some day, in some way, they will help and support you.

The true meaning of life is to plant trees under whose shade you do not expect to sit. *Nelson Henderson*

Susan Jeffers, author of *Feel the Fear and Do it Anyway,* says, "If getting is your motivation for giving, you worry about not getting anything back. Then you worry about not getting back *enough*. Your fear of being shortchanged or taken advantage of destroys your peace of mind."

The more nice things you do for others, the more **oomph** you give yourself. In fact, *you* will get whatever you want if you help enough people get whatever *they* want.

When you help someone's boat across a river, you'll find your own boat has reached the shore too.

#2 Don't put personal relationships on "automatic pilot."

Being emotionally and physically intimate with another person is hard work and there is always the temptation to put your relationship on "automatic pilot." Don't! Because if you do, you may fly okay for awhile, but sooner or later, the inattention and neglect will cause a crash! You have to stay awake.

Relationship expert Dr. J. Allan Peterson says 69% of married people simply take each other for granted and do not work at building their marriages. He says the average husband has the attitude of, "Why do you have to chase the bus once you've caught it?" And the average wife has the attitude of, "Once you've caught the fish, you throw away the bait." Motivational speaker Dr. Alan R. Zimmerman says with that kind of attitude toward relationships, it's no wonder people grow older and find out they only have one thing in common: they just happened to be married on the same day!

Be constantly aware of your partner's changing needs and then work to help meet them. Turn off the cruise control so you can steer your relationship in the direction *you* want it to go.

The happiest lovers are not the most realistic, but the most **positive.** They idealize their partners and **expect** their relationships to survive hard times. *Martin E. P. Seligman*

#3 Make people feel appreciated, important and admired

Psychologist Abraham Maslow, the "Father of Self-Actualization," said all human beings have the same three ego needs: the need to feel appreciated, the need to feel admired and the need to feel important. These needs are not equal, and they are met by other people.

Think about it. How do you feel when someone asks you for your opinion? How do you feel when someone admires your new tie or new haircut? These actions trigger positive feelings; but the reverse holds true, too. How do you feel if you do something nice for someone and they DON'T thank or even acknowledge you? How do you feel if a friend is repeatedly late for a lunch date?

Relationship counselor Dr. Ellen Kreidman says we fall in love because of how the other person makes us *feel* about ourselves and we get divorced because we no longer feel that way. She also believes that people have affairs because their spouse no longer says or does things to make them feel appreciated, admired or important; but someone *else* does!

To re-energize your relationships, always keep those three needs in mind when interacting with family, friends, clients, colleagues and customers.

Husbands are like fires. They go out if left unattended. *Zsa Zsa Gabor*

Make people feel appreciated:

When I called USAirways to change an upcoming flight, my call was placed on hold. Nothing unusual about that. But what made *this* call different is what I heard next: "Hi! I'm Dave Siegel, President and CEO of USAirways. One of my colleagues will be with you soon. Thanks for flying USAirways. We really appreciate your business!"

That personal message *did* make me feel appreciated and I didn't mind waiting a few more minutes.

Research shows that a business will lose 32% of its customers because they move, die, can get it cheaper some place else, or just want to try something different.

But the remaining 68% go elsewhere because they feel the people they deal with are indifferent to them and their needs.

You can never over-thank another person!

Ask yourself:

- When was the last time I told a client I appreciate them and their business?
- When was the last time I thanked my partner for making dinner?
- When was the last time I said thank you to the janitor or housekeeping staff for cleaning my office?
- When was the last time I thanked my children for playing so nicely with each other?

If you have to give business cards to your good customers, you haven't seen them enough.

Make people feel admired:

I believe we "*pay* someone a compliment," because compliments always pay dividends. So, look for opportunities to pay the people you know or meet a sincere compliment. A simple "You look good in blue," "You did a great job in the staff meeting" or "I like your hair that way" is an easy way to boost another person's **oomph**.

> People ask for criticism, but they only want praise.
>
> *W. Somerset Maugham*

I realized the power of a compliment when I went to a local rug gallery to look for a small rug for the entry hall of our new house. I wanted to spend up to $200, but after looking at a few price tags, I realized there was nothing in my price range. As I started to leave, a young man came over and introduced himself. "I am Chad Barati, the new owner of this store. May I help you?" Now, I didn't want to say, "Sorry, Chad, I can't afford anything in here!" So, I asked instead if he had any flat-woven rugs called kilims. He replied, "Oh! You know about kilims? That's very good! Yes, I have only a couple beautiful kilims over here that I bought just for those few, discriminating buyers with excellent taste who appreciate their special beauty. Let me show you my favorite one..."

Discriminating buyer? Excellent taste? Before he had even finished unrolling that carpet, I said, "I'll take it!" That beautiful kilim rug is now in our dining room, but the rest of the room remains empty because that one rug cost more than the money we had budgeted for an entire set of new dining room furniture!

DO THIS!

Write down the last three compliments and to whom you paid them:

Person: ____________________
Compliment: ____________________

Person: ____________________
Compliment: ____________________

Person: ____________________
Compliment: ____________________

Beginning tomorrow, pay a sincere compliment to three different people every day.

Make people feel important:

Since leaving the Louisville Mayor's Office, where I worked for over ten years, instead of telling people, "Now I work at home," I find it far more impressive to tell people: "I own the building where my business is located!" We *all* need to feel important!

Starting today, pretend that every person you meet has a sign that reads, **"Make me feel important."**

One way to do that is to ask people their opinion and

then really *listen* to the answer. Sometimes, instead of really listening to another person, I catch myself thinking about what I'm going to say *next*. So I remind myself that the same six letters in the word **LISTEN** also spell **SILENT**. Do your best to **silence** your thoughts, paraphrase back what you hear and give the other person 100% of your attention.

I also remind myself not to play the "Top It" game. That's when someone brags about an achievement and the other person tries to surpass it. We've all played the game. Maybe a co-worker brags about their child making the honor roll and you reply your child has been chosen valedictorian. I try to avoid the game when hearing about friends' vacations although I want so *badly* to say, "Let me tell you about MY trip!"

Another way to make others feel important is to keep them in the loop and ask their opinion. If you say to an employee, " I would appreciate your feed-back on these upcoming company changes," you empower that person and make them feel that they and their opinions are important.

Show respect for the other person's opinion. Never say, "You're wrong." *Dale Carnegie*

Dr. Carnegie also observed a person's name is the sweetest word in the language. People feel bigger and better when called by name because it is their most unique and valuable possession. So, make a special effort to remember people's names. The next time you meet someone, say the person's name aloud to imprint in on your brain. Then say it again at least three times during the next hour to *store* it.

I also use "sir" and "ma'am" when talking to anyone, regardless of their age or whether they're the company CEO or the janitor. It's remarkable how service improves when you simply say "No, ma'am" or "Yes, sir" when talking to customer service providers.

DO THIS!

Complete these sentences:

I would like to re-energize my relationship with:

____

I can make him/her feel appreciated by: ____________

____

I can make him/her feel important by: ____________

____

I can make him/her feel admired by: ____________

____

#4 Look for the lesson you can learn from difficult people

I come across different types of difficult people because I travel so much for business. Airport, restaurant or hotel staff, fellow travelers, and sometimes my seminar participants can be classic bullies, whiners, or know-it-alls. After years of being annoyed by these difficult behaviors, I came to realize:

☞ **Difficult people are difficult because it's working for them.**

☞ **You cannot change a difficult person**

With that in mind, instead of wasting my **oomph** being aggravated by difficult people, I now follow a few simple guidelines. I think they'll work for you, too.

First, I ask myself "Do I really **need** to deal with this person?" If the answer is no, then I leave them alone.

If the answer is "yes," then I ask myself two questions:

"What is my desired outcome from dealing with this person?" and "What skill or lesson can I learn from this person? Was this person put in my path to teach me patience or generosity or composure?"

Be kind to unkind people.
They need it the most.

Seen on a bumper sticker

Another tactic for dealing with difficult people is to look for the good that *must* be buried somewhere in them. There was a difficult co-worker in one of my previous jobs who could have been a valuable ally if I had just looked past her negative qualities and focused on her positive talents. Hindsight is always 20/20.

I never met a person I didn't like.... but sometimes I've got to look real hard. *Will Rogers*

DO THIS!

Name a difficult person you have to deal with personally or professionally: ______________________

Name five **positive** traits about that person:

____

____

____

____

____

Name the specific behavior you find difficult:

____

____

____

Name a skill you can practice when dealing with that person: ______________________

____

____

____

____

____

#5 Worry about what's right, not who's right!

I thought I married Mr. Right. I didn't realize his first name is Always.

I do an exercise in my seminars that dramatically illustrates how we are all naturally resistant when "pushed" by difficult people in our lives.

I have the entire room stand up, divide into pairs, and decide which person will be "red" and which person will be "blue." I then instruct the REDS to put their hands out in front of them, palms up, facing BLUE.

Next, I tell the BLUES: "Take your two hands and push hard on RED's hands—harder! Push harder!"

Then I tell them to stop pushing and ask, "When BLUE pushed on you, how many REDS immediately dropped their hands to their sides?" Usually, not even one person raises their hand! The laughter comes when I say:

"Hmmm...I think my instructions to REDS were: 'Put your hands out in front and turn and face BLUE.' I did NOT say: 'Keep them there no matter what!' 100% of the REDS resisted; in fact, you were all thinking, "They're not going to push ME down!"

And why do all the REDS resist? Because resistance is automatic! It's human nature: if someone pushes you, you push back! It's an automatic defensive reflex, like when the doctor hits your knee with a hammer, your foot kicks out. You don't think about it — it just happens!

"Pushing back" usually occurs when we're criticized. If a Know-it-All says you're doing something wrong and you argue with them, you are being resistant and actually holding them up. Remember: it takes *two* people to argue. Deepak Chopra says in *The Seven Spiritual Laws of Success*, "Any time you encounter resistance, recognize that if you force the situation, the resistance will only increase."

Peace of mind is better than giving them a piece of your mind.

J.P. MeEvoy

In the exercise, I ask the REDS, "What would have happened if you had dropped your hands when BLUE was pushing on you?" They respond: "BLUE would have fallen on their face!" When we argue, we "prop up" the other person.

Take the path of least resistance. The next time someone pushes on you, ask yourself, "In the grand scheme of things, how really important is it that I win this particular point? Should I spend my valuable **oomph** on this?"

It simply takes too much **oomph** to always be right! And always having to be right can create so much resentment, that you had better always be right, because you're building up a large contingency of people who can't wait to see you fall on your face!

If you just relinquish the need to defend your point of view, you will in that relinquishment gain access to enormous amounts of energy.

Deepak Chopra

#6 Learn to respond, not react

Have you ever said something in a heated moment that you immediately regretted? That's called reacting or speaking before thinking and it usually happens when someone has "pushed" you.

There is an important difference between reacting and responding. When you react, you speak first and then think about it. When you respond, you think first.... then speak. So, the difference between reacting and responding is about two seconds. That's how long you should wait before opening your mouth when someone has criticized you or pushed one of your "hot buttons."

Real human freedom is the ability to pause between the events of our lives and choose how we will respond. *Rollo May*

If the Know-It-All says, "That's not the way to do it," don't immediately open your mouth and reply, "Don't you tell me what to do!" That's a reaction, and it will immediately escalate the conflict. The right response would be to pause, smile and then respond: "Thank you for your input." Objectively evaluate their input and then do what *you* think is right.

If your boss asks in a hostile tone of voice, "Why did you do it *this* way?" Take a deep breath, smile and calmly respond, "How did you want me to do it?" The key is to be curious and not defensive. Always remember:

> Other people don't upset us. It is our *reaction* to other people that upsets us. *Susan Miller*

Tara Bennett-Goleman, author of *Emotional Alchemy: How the Mind Can Heal the Heart* explains, "According to neuroscience, there is a magic quarter-second between the impulse to act and the act itself." That passing instant is "a crucial point during which we can reject a self-defeating emotional impulse." A quarter-second doesn't seem very long, but it gives you just enough time to decide *not* to tell the boss where he can put his criticism! After you short-circuit your instinctive reaction, you still have a couple seconds to take a breath and smile before you calmly respond.

#7 Accept people exactly as they are.

This doesn't mean you have to like them all the time. Just accept them. Especially your spouse. They say a woman marries a man expecting he will change, but he doesn't. A man marries a woman expecting she won't change, but she does!

Even after fourteen years of marriage, I still want to change my husband instead of accepting him exactly as he is. I love him madly, yet I catch myself saying, "Why don't you..." or "I wish you would..." To change this really useless attitude, I just remind myself of the many things I'm sure Steve would love to change about *me*!

A man read an article to his wife that said women use 30,000 words a day and men only use 15,000.

The wife replied, "The reason has to be because a woman has to say everything twice."

The man turned to his wife and said, "What?"

DO THIS!

- For the next twenty-four hours, refrain from judging or criticizing anybody or anything.
- If that's too difficult, try to practice non-judgment for just the next hour!

It's like magic. When you live by yourself, all your annoying habits are gone! *Merrill Markoe*

#8 Be careful what you say!

A friend e-mailed me these great "How to Communicate with your Spouse" rules.

(Men: ignore them at your peril!)

Dangerous: What's for dinner?
Safer: Can I help you with dinner?
Safest: Where would you like to go for dinner?

Dangerous: Are you wearing THAT?
Safer: Gee, you look good in brown.
Safest: Wow! Look at you!

Dangerous: Should you be eating that?
Safer: You know, there are lots of apples left.
Safest: Can I get you a glass of wine with that?

Dangerous: What did you do all day?
Safer: I hope you didn't overdo it today.
Safest: I've always loved you in that robe.

#9 Don't take it personally!

When we take criticism personally, instead of seeing it as a problem that needs to be fixed, the problem becomes bigger and takes *longer* to fix. View any criticism objectively, ask for clarification, focus on solutions and move on!

And don't create problems where they don't exist. I once presented a two-day seminar in Washington DC and became aware that a woman in the audience *never* smiled. In fact, every time I looked at her, she had a frown on her face. I thought to myself, "Darla must hate this seminar!"

No matter what I said or did, she *never* smiled. I noticed this because I use a good amount of humor in my programs and people typically laugh. So I was concerned and wondered if I had said something to offend her.

At the end of the second day, Darla was the last person to leave the room. She turned to me and, barely opening her mouth, said, "Susan, I just want you to know...this was the best seminar I have ever attended." What?! I was totally surprised and said to her, "Darla, I thought you *hated* the seminar because you never once smiled." She replied, "People tell me I need to smile more." Wow!

We talked some more and it turned out Darla was self-conscious about her teeth and had taught herself not to smile. She wasn't aware that, like one-third of the human population, her lips turn downward at the corners, so it looked like she was always frowning.

But I had taken her frown *personally*. I thought there was a problem and it was about *me!*

That incident taught me a valuable lesson and now, if someone in my audience doesn't smile, I don't think it's because of me (and I just assume they have bad teeth!)

#10 Find an excuse to send a (real) card or note

We all love receiving cards in the mail. And the hand-signed, addressed and stamped ones are even more cherished since e-mail has made it too easy to just send cyber-notes. Boost your **oomph** by sending real cards to your family, friends, co-workers, and clients. And don't think you have to send expensive cards to show "you care to send the very best." Joan Riehm, Deputy Mayor of Louisville, creates her own New Year's cards and writes a personal note in each. Joan's simple cards mean much more than fancy holiday cards where even the signature is embossed!

Cards and notes are an easy way to re-energize relationships. Start with the traditional occasions: birthday, anniversary, get well, Christmas and Hanukah. I look for funny or unusual cards while traveling and find shopping for greeting cards in airport gift shops is a great way to spend time waiting for my next flight.

Once you've got a stock of "all-occasion" cards, move on to more *creative* occasions. For example:

- Thanksgiving cards: "I am thankful you're my friend/ husband/wife/partner/ client/co-worker/customer/ boss."
- Half-birthday cards: I have always celebrated my half birthday (July 7) because my 'real" birthday (January 7) is so close to the holidays. I send half-birthday cards to friends whose birthdays are also too close to the holidays, or if I missed the big day six months earlier!
- Send lots of valentines and sign them, "Someone who thinks you're terrific!"

#11 Resign your position as Manager of the Universe

In other words, don't offer unsolicited advice and tell people what to do. If someone tells you his or her problems, don't respond with, " Well, all you've got to do is...." Instead ask, "So what do **you** think are your options?" Listen to what they say and then ask, "So what do you think is your **best** option?"

My seminar attendees often ask, "What's the best way to motivate my kids, or spouse to do what I want them to do?" I always have to answer, "You can't!" The reality is, no one can motivate another person. You can only show someone why it is to his or her BENEFIT to do what you suggest. People are motivated for <u>their</u> reasons; not yours.

People take different roads seeking fulfillment and happiness. Just because they're not on *your* road doesn't mean they've gotten lost. *H. Jackson Brown, Jr.*

For eleven years, I was an unofficial "big sister" to several at-risk kids. On weekends, I would take them to movies, out to lunch or the swimming pool. Whenever I stopped to get money from the ATM, I would ask the kids, "How am I able to get money from this 'money wall'?" They would dutifully recite, "Because you stayed in school, and you got good grades and then you got a job and the job pays you money and you put it in the bank and that's how you get money from the money wall."

Did I motivate these kids to stay in school, get good grades and then get a job? No! But I did show them the benefits of doing those things.

You can lead a horse to water, but you can't make it drink.... But you can feed it salt tablets!

It takes a lot of effort for me not to "manage the universe." When I bought my first home computer, I showed my husband how he could manage our finances, get current news and sports scores on the internet and I badgered him to use it. But he had no interest in my new "toy." Then a few months later, raccoons moved into our attic and drove us both nuts with their late-night antics.

One night, I returned home from a week on the road and Steve said he had something to show me. He shined a flashlight out the upstairs bathroom window and there in a cage on the sunroom roof was a raccoon. Steve had downloaded all kinds of information off the internet (the humane way to catch raccoons, where to buy a cage, what they like to eat, etc.) and took care of our raccoon problem.

Steve now uses the internet all the time. But, he began using the internet for HIS reasons—not mine!

I now remind myself **daily** that I am not Master of the Universe and I try to only solve my **own** problems.

#12 Schedule "date nights" with your sweetie

I am writing these paragraphs on my 14th wedding anniversary and thinking how, even after all these years, my husband and I still act like we're on our honeymoon. Now, I suspect some of that may be due to the fact my speaking schedule keeps me out of town several days or weeks a month. We've learned that absence DOES make the heart grow fonder!

Sex when you're married is like going to a 7-Eleven. There's not much variety, but at 3AM, it's always there. *Carol Leifer*

But, even before I became a frequent business traveler, our love life had **oomph** because we plan Date Nights— and I highly recommend them. You may ask, "But what about spontaneity?" Yes, unplanned moments also happen, but we find the anticipation of a planned Date Night makes it even more exciting!

The idea of Date Night is to optimize each of the five senses to create "peak sensory moments."

SIGHT

We have NO distracting clutter in our bedroom and we always light candles, even if Date Night is in the morning or afternoon.

TOUCH

We often soak in our outdoor hot tub and I love good body lotions and the best quality, really soft sheets.

SMELL

Most of the year we open the screen door to our bedroom balcony so we can smell the trees, honeysuckle, wisteria vines and fresh air.

TASTE

Steve cooks us a great dinner and I save my favorite desserts for those nights.

SOUND

We turn-up-the-volume of our favorite CD's and tapes.

But the most important ingredient of our love life recipe is **FUN.** Steve and I have ***FUN*** together! And we don't just wait until Date Night for hugs and kisses. In fact, a favorite game is "Kissing in the Kitchen" which always makes our dog Teddy run around us in circles, barking.

Try planning a Date Night with your sweetie and make it **fun**. One last tip: The ancient Chinese art of Feng Shui recommends lighting **red** candles for maximum romantic energy. It really works!

Life is not measured by the number of breaths we take, but by the moments that take our breath away. *George Carlin*

DO THIS!

Describe your peak sensory moments:

SIGHT: ______________________________

____

TOUCH: ______________________________

____

SMELL: ______________________________

____

TASTE: ______________________________

____

SOUND: ______________________________

____

FINISH THIS SENTENCE:
I will schedule a "Date Night" for: ______________

____

A Dozen Ways to Re-Energize Your Relationships

1. **When you meet someone, ask yourself, "How can I *help* this person?"**
2. **Don't put personal relationships on "automatic pilot."**
3. **Make people feel appreciated, important and admired.**
4. **Look for the lesson you can learn from difficult people.**
5. **Worry about *what's* right, not *who's* right.**
6. **Learn to respond, not react.**
7. **Accept people exactly as they are.**
8. **Be careful what you say!**
9. **Don't take it personally.**
10. **Find an excuse to send a (real) card or note.**
11. **Resign your position as Manager of the Universe.**
12. **Schedule "date nights" with your sweetie.**

Chapter Nine

Seven Strategies to Help Re-Energize Your Job

> Success is waking up in the morning and bounding out of bed because there's something out there that you love to do, that you believe in, that you're good at, and you can hardly wait to get at it again today.
>
> *Whit Hobbs*

Do *you* wake up each and every morning, bound out of bed and say, "I can't WAIT to get to work today!" No? Not happening for you? Then let's try a different question.

Do you feel like you're the poster child for burnout? Do you have a B.A. in Burnout? Is Burnout your middle name?

If you know all about burnout, then I have one word for you: **Congratulations!**

That's right! Be proud of your burnout because you cannot burnout without having first been on FIRE!

At some point, you were fired up about your job. Can you remember the interview you had for the position you are in? You got dressed up in your best clothes and confidently marched into that interview hoping to be hired by the company.

Now, six months or six years later you find yourself dragging out of bed and even complaining about your job or your supervisor. What changed? You did! Your attitude changed. Your perception of your job changed.

You were once on fire, and being on fire with enthusiasm is the difference between doing an okay job and an **outstanding** job... or sometimes even *getting* the job! And the first letter of outrageous and the first letter of outstanding are the first two letters of **oomph!**

If you want to go from "okay" to "outstanding" and have outrageous success, you need to recall the original enthusiasm you felt for your job and get re-energized.

Here are seven strategies to help you do just that:

#1 If you can't always love WHAT you do then love WHY you do it

If I asked you to answer in one word, "Why do you work?" you might say, **MONEY**!

And this is true. A paycheck is a powerful incentive to go to work each day. But, I believe we don't just work for the money; I believe we work for what we're going to **do with** the money!

It's not just about paying bills; it's about what those bills represent:

- your house/apartment/condo
- the electricity/water/telephone

- your new car
- your child's braces
- the family vacation to Disney World

This is **WHY** you work!

DO THIS!

Make a list of what you WANT:

I want to own: ____________________________

I want to go: ____________________________

I want my kids to own/go ____________________________

____

Get pictures of these things and put them where you can see them at work.

One reason *I* work is so I can take trips with my husband. In my office, I have pictures of where we've been (Greece, New Zealand, and Costa Rica) and where we **want** to go (Thailand, Japan, and Alaska).

Put pictures of that new car, house or Hawaii in constant, direct view and the next time you have one of those "they-can-take-this-job-and-shove-it" moments, look at these pictures and **remind yourself why you work!**

Disney World employees are told that whenever they don't *feel* like smiling to remember they get **paid** to smile. So remind yourself, "I'm being paid $_____ a week to put up with this."

Now you may be thinking, "But I don't work *just* for the money and what it can buy me. I work for the outcome and not the income." That's great! Although I am reminded of a bumper sticker I once saw:

Anyone who says money can't buy happiness, just doesn't know where to shop!

There **are** many other perks of working, including socializing, sense of accomplishment and feeling you're making a difference.

My sister Kathy is a second grade teacher and she earns a pretty puny salary for being part-time parent, counselor, nurse and encourager to 25 kids. But she says you can't put a price tag on the joy she feels when one of her students finally discovers how to read.

To love what you do and feel that it matters—how could anything be more fun? *Katherine Graham*

DO THIS!

Write down all the things you enjoy about your job (other than the paycheck!) ______________________________

____

Keep this list next to the picture of your dream vacation and review it daily (especially if they announce a salary freeze!)

#2 Solve people's problems

We are paid in direct proportion to the value of the problems we solve. Minimum wage employees make minimum wage because they solve problems that require minimum expertise. Highly paid people make the big bucks because the problems they solve require *maximum* expertise.

What kind of problems do *you* solve? If you're not happy with the money you're making, then you aren't solving big enough problems!

The key to outrageous business success is to find a problem and solve it. In each and every phone call you make or receive from a client or customer, you should ask, " What are your problems and how can I help?"

Ask yourself a simple question, "If I was a prospect, client or customer for **my** own services, what problems would **I** want solved?" Make a long list.

When solving any problem, first ask yourself whether or not there is a completely different way of approaching the problem. Try the unexpected and break the habit of your habits. Perhaps you should be doing exactly the *opposite* of what you are doing today.

> **The definition of insanity is doing the same thing over and over and expecting different results.**
>
> *Albert Einstein*

When you solve a problem at work, write it down. There is nothing your boss likes more than to not have to solve another problem. You should keep track of the problems you probably solve on a daily basis and consolidate them on an Accomplishments List you present to your boss during your annual review. You might say, "I solved a personnel problem by creating a flex schedule when an administrative assistant was on an eight week medical leave." Also, point out that you saved your company money because they didn't have to hire a temp!

Be perceived as a problem-solver, not a "problem child!"

#3 Resolve conflicts you have with co-workers

According to a University of North Carolina survey, 53% of respondents said they lost work time worrying about a past or future confrontation with a co-worker. 37% said a hostile confrontation caused them to reduce their commitment to the organization. 28% said they lost work time because they avoided the person with whom they had a confrontation. And 22% said they put less effort into their work because of a confrontation with a co-worker.

Have you ever found yourself in a similar situation? Unresolved conflict sucks **oomph** from the workplace. If you are a manager, this survey should be especially troubling because of its effect on productivity.

If you personally have an unresolved conflict with a co-worker, first, acknowledge it; re-read Chapter Four about **Oomph** Busters for specific ways to handle the conflict, and do what **you** can to resolve it.

And resist the temptation to join Blame Storming and its evil twin Malicious Gossip when they visit your workplace. Blame Storming is when you sit around in a group and discuss why a deadline was missed or a project failed and *who was responsible*.

Malicious Gossip is any form of communication that harms another person. Both are **oomph** busters and can be deadly. Remember that fact-finding is always a better use of your time than fault-finding.

When you throw dirt, all you do is lose ground.

#4 Listen to your inner clock

Did you know employees are more likely to reach their peak performance and productivity on Tuesdays? According to a survey by a California temporary staffing service, Friday is the *least* productive day.

That was news to me; however, I do know that everybody works best at different *times* of the day. Although your job may require you to be at your desk from 9 to 5, you probably do your **best** work during a certain segment of each day.

Are you a morning or afternoon person? After decades of working both for other people and for myself, I now realize, I am a "midday person." Whether writing a report, or writing this book, I have always done my quality work between the hours of 11:00am and 4:00pm. This means I rarely "do lunch," instead, I meet friends for coffee and then use the caffeine rush to work through the afternoon.

> The rule is simple: Anything you consider unpleasant do first. Get it behind you. *Rick Pitino*

Determine what times during the day you have the most **oomph** and plan your day accordingly. Make an appointment with yourself, close your door and do not allow interruptions or uninvited visitors for one hour each day. If you always set aside what you're doing to attend to someone else's needs, you convey the message it's okay to interrupt you. Tell people you're "on a deadline" and don't tell them what the deadline is!

Also, keep an inventory of tasks that require the least amount of **oomph** or mental effort like data input, reading professional magazines or just ordering supplies. Match your productivity level to your **oomph** level.

We all have times when we think more effectively and times when we shouldn't be thinking at all.

Daniel Cohen

DO THIS!

I have the most energy at_____:00am and/or _____:00pm.

What I usually do during those times is:

___:00am __________________________________

___:00pm __________________________________

Starting this week, what I WILL do is:

___:00am __________________________________

___:00pm __________________________________

I work for myself, which is fun, except when I call in sick, I know I'm lying. *Rita Rudner*

#5 Do something different

Since graduating from college, I have taught English and drama to grades 5-12, directed college drama productions, owned a balloon delivery business, managed public relations for the city library system, was an assistant to the Mayor of Louisville, Kentucky in charge of special events, organized festivals and events for private clients, and created my own speaking and training company called Re-Energizing Communications Inc.

When I get tired of what I'm currently doing, I'll do something else. Just like my houseplants, when I feel root-bound, I re-pot myself in order to grow.

The Department of Labor says, on average, we will have four different jobs before the age of 30. This was not our parent's norm. After college, my father worked his way up the corporate ladder from clerk to vice-president at the same Chicago food brokerage company where he worked until his retirement. That type of job stability rarely happens in today's world of company mergers.

If you enjoy what you do, you'll be successful. And if you don't enjoy what you do, you won't be successful. Work is reward, not punishment. So, if or when you feel root-bound, trust your instincts and move on to your next career.

Fall in love with what you do for a living. I'd rather be a failure at something I love than be successful at something I hate. *George Burns*

#6 Identify your next position

Even if you have just started your current position, you need to identify the job or position you want *next*.

DO THIS!

1. Write down your current job title or classification:

____

____

2. Write down your NEXT job title (it may be "retired"!)

____

____

3. Next, write down the specific skills, experience, or education that is required for that next position:

____

____

____

____

____

To get re-energized in your *current* position, think about what you can do on the job that will help get you to your *next* position. If you're a lower level administrative assistant and the next higher level requires that you know how to create an Excel® spreadsheet, then find someone to teach you, preferably at work during your breaks. Offer to teach them one of your expert skills like how to create a PowerPoint presentation.

That's called trading expert skills. And then, you're not just going to work every day; you're going to your "on-the-job *training*" — and they're *paying* you to learn!

Find something you like to do so much you'd gladly do it for nothing; then learn to do it so well people are happy to pay you for it. *Walt Disney*

#7 Create allies, not adversaries

My friend Dolores Triplett once told me, "Be careful whose toe you step on today because it might be attached to the derriere you have to kiss tomorrow!" Another way of expressing this great advice is: "What goes around, comes around."

A woman in one of my seminars related how a summer intern at her company had been treated rudely by the office manager. The intern was ordered to run personal errands for the manager and was belittled by her at staff meetings until summer was over and she returned to college.

Imagine the office manager's surprise when the intern re-appeared the following spring as a manager that **she** now had to report to! Turns out, the intern's uncle was a company vice-president and had promised his niece a manager's job once she had her college degree!

Don't burn bridges. You'll be surprised by how many times you have to cross the same river.

If you watch horse racing like I do here in Louisville, Kentucky at Churchill Downs, you'll notice the horse with the most people betting on it becomes the "favorite." The favorite is often the first horse to cross the wire and win the race. Therefore, if you want to be a winner, then you want lots of people betting on **you!**

The easiest way to be the winning favorite and to get people in your corner (to mix sports metaphors!) is to ask people for their help. When you ask someone to help you, you recognize his or her abilities and expertise. And they feel like they have an investment in your success.

Create a grandstand of allies encouraging you on to success, instead of a stadium of adversaries, who would rather see you stumble.

Seven Strategies to Re-Energize Your Job

1. **If you can't always love WHAT you do then love WHY you do it.**
2. **Solve people's problems.**
3. **Resolve conflicts you have with co-workers.**
4. **Listen to your inner clock.**
5. **Do something different.**
6. **Identify your next position.**
7. **Create allies, not adversaries.**

Chapter Ten

8 MORE Strategies to Re-Energize Your Job

Human beings and machines have something in common: they must be turned-on to work! And **oomph** is the ignition switch. People achieve what they want in direct proportion to how much enthusiasm they have for what they do.

It is not realistic to think you are **always** going to be on fire with enthusiasm for your job. I'm sure there are many days when you're lucky to just maintain a slow boil! However, you are going to work an average of 90,000 hours before you retire. So, here are eight more strategies to help you create greater job satisfaction.

#1 Fire your boss

I often ask my seminar audiences these questions: "How many of you work for one boss?" A few people will raise their hands.

"How many of you work for multiple bosses?" A few more people raise their hands.

Finally, I ask:

"How many of you work for one boss with multiple personalities?"

Almost everyone raises his or her hand!

Everyone has mood swings and you can't expect your boss to always be perfect and predictable. However, as I said in Chapter Two, if your boss is a Neg-a-holic, you need to find a different boss. If your boss *constantly* complains about the company, the other employees, the job you are doing, his or her home-life, or lack thereof, company policies or *their* boss, then it's a chronic condition that will not improve with time.

Negative people do not want solutions to their problems, so don't waste your **oomph** trying to make things better. It's an impossible task. And do not underestimate the effect your boss's negative attitude has on you.

Business philosopher Jim Rohn says the most important question to ask on the job is not, "What am I getting?" The most important question to ask is, "What am I becoming?" I often hear about horribly negative bosses from my seminar attendees and how miserable they feel as a result of exposure to them.

Your boss is the single most influential person to your career success and happiness. You don't need to be "best friends" with your boss; in fact, you should draw a clear line between your personal and professional lives! But if you find yourself tolerating rudeness, harassment of any sort, or constant, enervating negativity, find yourself a new boss or find yourself a new job.

If you love what you do, you'll never have to work a day of your life. *Confucius*

#2 Take your job seriously, but take yourself lightly

If you follow all the rules, you miss all the fun. *Katherine Hepburn*

I was on a small commuter flight which typically has pre-recorded safety procedures I tend to ignore simply because I've heard them so often. This flight was different.

The flight attendant took the microphone and said, "There may be fifty ways to leave your lover, but there are only three ways to leave this aircraft. In the event of a sudden loss of pressure, masks will drop. Stop screaming, put on your mask, and if you are traveling with two children, decide now which one you love more." By this time, all of the passengers were laughing.

During the flight, she continued to chat with the people in the front rows and as we were about to land, she announced, "We'd like to thank you for flying with us today. And the next time you get the insane urge to go blasting through the skies in a pressurized metal tube, we hope you'll think of us here at United Express."

The entire cabin gave her a round of applause.

The flight attendant took her job seriously, but she still made the flight fun for herself and her passengers.

Laughter is the shortest distance between two people. *Victor Borge*

If you or your workplace has a terminal case of seriousness, lighten up! A study by *HR Focus* found organizations that integrate fun into work have lower levels of absenteeism, increased productivity and less downtime.

Here are some suggestions to add some fun to your workplace:

- When you arrive at your job in the morning let the first thing you say brighten everyone's day.
- If you have a long hallway, have a Friday afternoon bowling party or set-up a miniature golf course through the cubicles.
- Rent a karaoke machine for your next office party.
- Have staff meeting "show and tell" time to report accomplishments and pass around vacation pictures.
- Keep Lifesaver candies on hand for helpful co-workers.
- Domino's Pizza has "bring-your-pet-to-work days" (hopefully they don't hold this event where they make the pizzas!)

All I wanna do is have some fun. I've got a feeling I'm not the only one. *song lyrics by Sheryl Crow*

☞ Put smile-makers in your workspace

Bring in some pictures of your kids, your husband, wife, partner, dog, cat, etc. and put them where you can see them.

Photos taken by professional photographers are fine, but what works best are those special candid shots that evoke great memories.

On the wall next to my computer are pictures of my niece Stephanie with blueberry pie smeared on her face, my husband on a Swiss mountain, my niece Caroline with our dog, and my entire family at my dad's 80th birthday party. I can't *help* but smile when I look at these photos.

No appointment necessary.
We'll hear you coming.

Sign on a muffler shop

Here are other smile-makers you can display to give yourself an **oomph** boost when you need it:

- Notes of praise from your boss
- Thank you notes and cards
- Postcards from favorite vacation places
- Cartoons that always make you laugh

To avoid clutter and make the items more special, rotate them rather than displaying them all at once.

#3 Learn to "Satis-fice"

I needed to create a simple slide for an upcoming seminar. Even with my limited computer experience, it should have taken no more than 15-20 minutes. Wrong! It took me over an hour to make that one simple slide because I started "tweaking" it: I changed the type font, font size; then I tried boxing the title, and I really got into trouble when I began changing the colors! I wasted valuable **oomph** because I didn't "satis-fice." That word is in the latest edition of the Random House Dictionary. It means: "to satisfy and suffice."

Do you still need to proofread your documents? Absolutely! Never rely just on spell-check. A woman who worked for the Dayton Chamber of Commerce told me about the time they had to throw away 5000 full-color brochures because spell-check didn't notice the typist had left the "**L**" out of the Department of **Public** Works!

"Tweaking" and fine-tuning beyond a reasonable amount are time and **oomph** wasters.

#4 Stay Focused!

Does the following scenario sound familiar?

One morning as I was just starting my writing, I turned on the desk lamp and discovered the light bulb had burned out, so I went to the kitchen to find a new one, noticed the dog's water dish needed filling so I filled it, then emptied the dishwasher so I could load it with the glasses that were in the sink, turned on the TV "to watch a littl CNN," went outside to get the mail, talked to my next-door neighbor, came back inside, opened the mail and read two articles in *Organic Gardening* magazine, returned to my office to go on-line to find a website mentioned in the magazine, checked my e-mail, wrote five replies and forwarded two items of interest, edited my e-mail address book and then stayed on-line the rest of the afternoon looking for hotels for our upcoming trip to Italy until it became dark and I <u>really</u> needed the lamp I had tried to turn on earlier!

The above scenario is one reason why it took me over four years to finish this book. I succumbed to the effects of

AAADD (Age-Activated Attention Deficit Disorder) and failed to stay focused on the task at hand.

> Nothing can add more power to your life than concentrating all of your energies on a limited set of targets. *Nido Qubein*

To help solve this problem, I wrote, "STAY FOCUSED" on a neon yellow sticky note and it's on my computer monitor right now, staring me in the face. A simple solution, yet it somehow keeps me focused each time I get distracted.

DO THIS!

Distractions in my work environment are: ____________

____

____

I can eliminate these distractions by: ____________

____

____

#5 Always be planning your NEXT vacation

My husband has worked in the same department at the University of Louisville Hospital for thirty years. One advantage to his long tenure is, he gets *lots* of vacation time.

I know many people who prefer to use vacation time for home-improvement projects, and that's great! But *our* motto is, "If you don't go, you won't know." So whenever we can, we get out of town. If we're not on a trip, we're planning the next one because we know we won't go anywhere *unless* we plan it. And actually, I enjoy planning our vacations almost as much as going on them!

Whether you enjoy traveling like we do, or whether your idea of the perfect vacation is to do NOTHING, always know when your next vacation is and what you have to look forward to. And think about getting away from home during your vacation, even if it's for a quick overnight trip.

DO THIS!

Write here WHEN your next vacation is: ____________

____

Write here WHAT you want to do during that time:

____

____

____

Write WHERE you would like to go: ____________

____

____

____

Put pictures of your "dream vacation" on your desk or bulletin board so you can always see them!

#6 See yourself as a free agent selling your skills for a fee

Do you see yourself as just an employee working for your employer for a paycheck? Well, how you perceive yourself is how *others* will perceive *you*. I tell administrative assistants if they think, "I'm just a secretary," then they will be perceived as "just a secretary," treated like "just a secretary" and paid like they are "just a secretary!"

A more valuable self-image is, "I am an independent contractor selling my skills to this company for a fee." This self-perception does not mean you aren't loyal to your current employer or not a team player. It means you recognize the temporary nature of many jobs in this time of mergers, layoffs and corporate restructuring.

No matter who signs your paycheck, in the final analysis, you work for yourself. *Glenn Van Ekeren*

See yourself as a free agent selling your skills for a fee and remember, the more skills, the higher the fee you can command. As an independent contractor, you need to take charge of your own morale. Don't expect the company to inspire, excite or reward you more than you are worth to them.

DO THIS!

1. Take inventory of your skills:
   If I asked your boss to list your strengths and skills, what would be on that list? ____________________

   ____

   ____

   If I asked your best friend, spouse or family members to list your strengths and skills, what would be on their list? ____________________

   ____

   ____

   What strengths and skills would *you* add to those lists?

   ____

   ____

2. Take what you just wrote and make a Master List. Write: "I am: ______________________________"
   and list all your strengths.

   Write: "I can: ______________________________"
   and list your skills.

   Don't be modest. This is who you are! And when someone says, "You're a real problem-solver," or "Thanks for being so helpful," add that strength or skill to your list.

3. Learn what your skills are worth in your city or state by checking www.salary.com.

4. Put your skills list where you can see it whenever you need some extra **oomph**.

- When you make a mistake, read the list.
- When you have a self-doubt, read the list.
- Before you go on a first date, read the list.
- Before you go to a job interview, read the list.

#7 Venting is Good ...but NOT at work!

I don't cook, but I do understand the principle behind a pressure cooker: if you don't vent the steam, the cooker will explode! You are just like that pressure cooker, especially if you have a high-stress job.

It's *healthy* to let off steam about the boss's nitpicking, the company's latest pay policy, the annoying co-worker; but don't vent at work! Wait until you're safely in your car, and then recite every little thing that drove you absolutely crazy that day.

It's okay to occasionally say to co-workers: "I'm having a crazy day!" But save the real complaints for later. Why?

1. Because complaining to co-workers won't get results or solve your problems.
2. Because negative people don't get promoted.

Anyone who thinks he or she is indispensable should stick a finger in a glass of water and notice how long the hole stays there after the finger is removed.

When pressures build up, write an angry e-mail; but play it safe and don't type the recipient's name on it. And don't send it! Just type the e-mail and let off some steam.

Don't tell people at work your problems. Instead, while driving home, pretend a co-worker is sitting next to you in the car and let loose with everything that is driving you nuts. Recite *all* your problems, and if you get home before the list is finished, drive around the block a few times, because your partner doesn't really want to hear them either!

DO THIS!

1. Get yourself a "Venting Buddy," preferably someone who doesn't work with you so they can listen objectively to your problems without inserting their own opinions ("Oh yeah, I can't stand her either!"). My Venting Buddy is: ____________________

2. Establish venting rules:

   - The venter is allowed two minutes of uninterrupted venting (in other words, the listener may not open his or her mouth for at least two minutes).
   - The listener may ONLY sympathize with the venter.
   - The listener may NOT offer advice ("Just tell them where they can put that job!")
   - After a maximum of five minutes, the venter and listener switch roles.

There! Don't you feel better?

#8 Focus on the positive— not the negative

> Write the bad things that are done to you in sand, but write the good things that happen to you on a piece of marble.
>
> ***Arabic Parable***

If you receive a performance review or annual evaluation that has all "excellents" and only ONE "needs improvement," what do you usually focus on? That's right! The one "needs improvement!" We all tend to lose sight of how well we're doing when faced with any criticism.

I once spoke to a group of two hundred people in Toronto and almost all of the program evaluations that day were highly complimentary. Except one. One person gave me a low score and wrote, "Susan talked too much about God." Instead of focusing on the 199 "highly satisfied" attendees that day, I obsessed about that ONE dissatisfied person! I even eliminated all references to God from subsequent programs, until I finally realized the pendulum had swung too far the other way.

I now mention my faith in my programs, and if I get another complaint, I'll just say a prayer for that person!

How would you like it when every time *you* make a mistake, a big red light goes on and 18,000 people boo? *Jaques Plante, former hockey goalie*

Speaker and author Linda Larsen suggests a great way to get your entire workplace to focus on the positive and not the negative.

- ☞ **Post a large mat board on the wall with a heading that says: WHAT'S RIGHT TODAY?**
- ☞ Ask people to find three right things they notice other people doing during the day.
- ☞ They jot down what they saw on a Post-it® note and stick it on the board.

What happens is people actually start looking for what's right—and therefore *see* lots more right things.

And finally, if you feel your initial enthusiasm for your job waning, once again focus on its positive aspects by reminding yourself why you accepted the job in the first place. You must have had good reasons for taking it. What were they?

DO THIS!

Write down as many reasons as you can remember for accepting your current position.

____

____

____

____

____

Write down three work-related accomplishments that you are most proud of:

1. ______________________________________

2. ______________________________________

3. ______________________________________

When you receive *any* work-related criticism, step back and review the criticism objectively. Then read this list and spend as much time reviewing *this* list as you do re-hashing the criticism.

8 *More* Ways to Re-Energize Your Job

1. **Fire your boss.**
2. **Take your job seriously, but take yourself lightly.**
3. **Learn to "Satis-fice."**
4. **Stay focused.**
5. **Always be planning your next vacation.**
6. **See yourself as a free agent.**
7. **Venting is good...but not at work.**
8. **Focus on the positive—not the negative.**

Postscript

I sincerely hope you found ***Oomph Power!*** to be:

- ✔ Helpful
- ✔ Fun
- ✔ Encouraging
- ✔ And, most of all, thought-provoking

Please share anything you learned from this book with someone else and share your comments and outrageous success stories with **me** at: **Susan@oomphpower.com**

And one final thought:

> Outrageous success isn't a destination, it's a journey. So enjoy the ride and do it with **oomph**! *Susan Miller*

Bibliography and Suggested Reading

Allen, David, *Getting Things Done*, New York, Penguin Books, 2001.

Bennett-Goleman, Tara, *Emotional Alchemy: How the Mind Can Heal the Heart,* New York, Harmony Books, 2001.

Boothman, Nicholas, *How to Make People Like You*, New York: Workman Publishing, 2000.

Carlson, Richard, *Don't Sweat the Small Stuff at Work*, New York: Hyperion, 1998.

Chopra, Deepak, *The Seven Spiritual Laws of Success*, San Rafael: Amber-Allen Publishing, 1994.

Covey, Stephen R. *The 7 Habits of Highly Effective People*, New York: Simon & Schuster, 1989.

Ferrari, Joseph, *Procrastination and Task Avoidance*, New York: Plenum Publications, 1995.

Foster, Jack, *How to Get Ideas*, San Francisco: Berrett-Koehler Publishers, 1996.

Hemseth, Dave and Yerkes, Leslie, *301 Ways to Have Fun at Work*. San Francisco, Berrett-Koehler Publishers Inc. 1997.

Jeffers, Susan, *Feel the Fear and Do it Anyway*, New York: Fawcett Books, 1998.

Kleiner, Susan, *Power Eating*, Champaign: Human Kinetics, 1998.

Larsen, Linda, *True Power*, Sarasota: Brandywine Publishing, 2000.

Lavington, Camille, *You've Only Got Three Seconds*, New York: Main Street Books, 1997.

McGraw, Phillip C. *Life Strategies*, New York: Hyperion, 1999.

Peters, Tom, *The Pursuit of WOW!* New York: Vintage Books, 1994.

Pitino, Rick, *Success is a Choice*, New York: Broadway Books, 1997.

Runion, Meryl, *Power Phrases*, Cascade: Power Potentials, 2002.

Schwartz, David J. *The Magic of Thinking Success*, Hollywood: Wilshire Book Company, 1987.

Seligman, Martin, *Learned Optimism*, New York: Pocket Books, 1998.

Sher, Barbara, *Live the Life You Love*, New York: Delacorte Press, 1996.

Silber, Lee, *Career Management for the Creative Person*, New York: Three Rivers Press, 1999.

Temme, Jim, *Productivity Power*, Mission, KS: SkillPath Publications, 1993.

Thompson, Charles "Chic," *What a Great Idea!* New York: Harper Collins, 1992.

Tracy, Brian, *Maximum Achievement*, New York: Fireside, 1993.

Van Ekeeren, *12 Simple Secrets of Happiness at Work*, Paramus: Prentice Hall Press, 2001.

Winget, Larry, *The Simple Way to Success*, Tulsa: Win Publications! 1996.

Zukav, Gary, *The Seat of the Soul*, New York: Fireside, 1989.

About the Author

SUSAN MILLER is an international speaker, corporate trainer and President of Re-Energizing Communications Inc. Susan's award-winning speeches and seminars have re-energized audiences throughout the United States, Canada and Australia.

A native of Evanston, Illinois, Susan holds a Bachelor of Arts degree in Education and Theatre from Indiana University, a Master of Arts degree in Education and a Master of Science degree in Library Science from Spalding University. She also holds a "B.A. in Burn-Out."

Susan has been a teacher, small business owner, Director of Special Programs and Events for the City of Louisville, Kentucky and a one-time-only bungee-jumper.

An in-demand speaker and seminar leader, Susan addresses thousands of people each year at association and corporate meetings and conventions. Her high energy, high content programs on motivation, stress management and communication skills get groups involved, laughing and learning.

Susan lives with her husband and their dog beside the Ohio River in Louisville, Kentucky.

If you would like Susan to add some **Oomph Power!** to your next meeting, please contact her at:

Web site: www.susanmillerspeaks.com

Mail: Re-Energizing Communications, Inc.
P.O. Box 1169
Prospect, KY 40059-1169

Toll-free: 1-8-NOT-BORING

Give *Oomph Power!* to Your Friends and Colleagues

Order Form

❑ YES, I want ____ copies of *Oomph Power!* for $14.95 each.
(Please call for quantity discounts for more than ten copies.)

❑ YES, I am interested in having Susan speak or give a seminar to my company, association or organization. Please send me information.

Please include $4.95 shipping/handling for your entire order.
Kentucky residents must include 6% sales tax and Canadian orders must include 7% GST. Payment must accompany orders.

❑ My check or money order for $ ________ is enclosed.

❑ Please charge my:

❑ Visa ❑ MasterCard ❑ American Express

Name ______________________________

Organization ______________________________

Address ______________________________

City/State/Zip ______________________________

Phone ______________________________

E-mail ______________________________

Card # ______________________ Exp. Date___/___/___

Signature ______________________________

Mail Orders: *Please make your check payable and return to:*
Re-Energizing Communications, Inc.
PO Box 1169
Prospect, KY 40059-1169

Telephone Orders: toll-free 1-8-NOT-BORING (1-866-826-7464)
Fax Orders: 502-228-6272
On-line Orders: www.oomphpower.com

Thank you for your order!